T0328799

Cambridge Elements ≡

Elements in the Philosophy of Immanuel Kant
edited by
Desmond Hogan
Princeton University
Howard Williams
University of Cardiff
Allen Wood
Indiana University

KANT'S THEORY OF LABOUR

Jordan Pascoe
Manhattan College

CAMBRIDGE
UNIVERSITY PRESS

Shaftesbury Road, Cambridge CB2 8EA, United Kingdom

One Liberty Plaza, 20th Floor, New York, NY 10006, USA

477 Williamstown Road, Port Melbourne, VIC 3207, Australia

314–321, 3rd Floor, Plot 3, Splendor Forum, Jasola District Centre,
New Delhi – 110025, India

103 Penang Road, #05–06/07, Visioncrest Commercial, Singapore 238467

Cambridge University Press is part of Cambridge University Press & Assessment,
a department of the University of Cambridge.

We share the University's mission to contribute to society through the pursuit of
education, learning and research at the highest international levels of excellence.

www.cambridge.org
Information on this title: www.cambridge.org/9781009165747

DOI: 10.1017/9781009165754

First published 2022

A catalogue record for this publication is available from the British Library.

ISBN 978-1-009-16574-7 Paperback
ISSN 2397-9461 (online)
ISSN 2514-3824 (print)

Kant's Theory of Labour

Elements in the Philosophy of Immanuel Kant

DOI: 10.1017/9781009165754
First published online: September 2022

Jordan Pascoe
Manhattan College
Author for correspondence: Jordan Pascoe, jordan.pascoe@manhattan.edu

Abstract: By exploring the innovative account of labour embedded in Kant's political philosophy, this Element develops an intersectional and materialist reading of Kant. Drawing on Kant's early notes and lectures on themes of labour, the household, sex, and slavery, alongside his political, historical, and anthropological writing on race and gender, Jordan Pascoe argues that Kant's normative account of independence is configured through his theory of labour, which attends in innovative ways to reproductive labour. By revealing the close linkages between slavery and domestic labour in Kant's political thought, Pascoe shows how Kant's evolving thinking about labour may have shaped his ultimate rejection of slavery, rather than any change in his theory of race. Instead, Kant's theory of labour provides a lens through which to read his anthropological accounts of race and gender as embedded within his political philosophy, and to develop an intersectional analysis of his practical philosophy.

This Element also has a video abstract: www.cambridge.org/pascoe

Keywords: Kant, intersectionality, labour, feminist philosophy, social reproduction

ISBNs: 9781009165747 (PB), 9781009165754 (OC)
ISSNs: 2397-9461 (online), 2514-3824 (print)

Contents

1 Could It Be Worth Thinking about Kant on Labour?

In a groundbreaking 1993 article on sex and marriage, Barbara Herman laid the foundation for feminist Kant scholarship that uses Kantian arguments to address a range of feminist quandaries;[1] inspired by Herman's willingness to open new Kantian doors, I ask what happens when we examine Kant's theory of labour, which runs through his political, anthropological, historical, and moral arguments.

Kant's theory of labour provides a framework to think beyond and between established divisions in Kant scholarship, illuminating elements of Kant's political arguments with implications for contemporary Kantian and feminist scholarship, as well as for debates about Kant's theory of race. This project develops an intersectional analysis of Kant (Crenshaw 1989) which invites dialogue across established methodological silos within Kant scholarship. As race and gender have moved towards the centre of Kantian scholarship in the last decade, they have remained strikingly distinct, with work on sex/gender taking up Kant's discussions of sex, marriage, caregiving, and citizenship, and work on race/racism focusing on his anthropological, geographical, and cosmo-politan texts.[2] This has led to an emerging discourse on the difficulty of intersectional approaches to Kant, which reflects Kant's own careful insistence on categorical thinking.[3]

Just as Herman's analysis of Kant and marriage invited contemporary feminists to attend to (surprising) resources within Kant's philosophy, my analysis of Kant's account of labour maps resources in Kant relevant to contemporary materialist, intersectional, decolonial, and social reproduction feminist theorizing, as well as to contemporary Black radical thought. By identifying patterns of institutionalized inequality within Kant's political thought, I develop an account of the intersectional political economy embed-ded in Kant's account of Right,[4] revealing foundational Kantian resources for theorizing patterns of dependency and oppression that challenge frameworks found in Locke, Hegel, and Marx.

---

[1] The genealogy of these arguments is expertly summarized in Varden 2020, especially pp. 20–6. Examples of these arguments can be found in Altman 2010, Denis 2001, Hay 2013, Kleingeld 1993, Langton 2009, Nussbaum 1995, O'Neill 1989, Papadaki 2007, Pascoe 2013, 2015, and 2018, Sabourin 2021, Schaff 2001, Schapiro 1999, and Varden 2006b, 2006a, and 2020.

[2] Where scholars have taken up these questions together, it is often by way of drawing a parallel. See, for example, Mendieta 2011, Mills 2005, Pateman, and Mills 2007, Kleingeld 2007 and 2014a.

[3] For engagements with the problem of intersectionality in Kant, see Huseyinzadegan 2018, Kleingeld 2019, Pascoe 2019a, Huseyinzadegan and Pascoe Forthcoming.

[4] I draw on Nancy Folbre's (2021) conceptualization of intersectional political economy. This argument is elaborated in Section 7.

I develop Kant's theory of labour across his political, anthropological, histor-ical, and moral texts, building on recent work developing the role of non-ideal theory in Kant's practical philosophy. To map the emergence of Kant's theory of labour and its relation to the development of his thinking about race, gender, sex, slavery, and colonialism, I go beyond the texts published in his lifetime, examining recently published notes and drafts in order to illuminate the ways that his evolving theories of race, coloniality, and slavery, his account of sex and marriage, his analysis of parenthood and servitude, his treatment of contract and trade, and his development of the relationship between citizenship and enlight-enment intersect and generate one another. My holistic analysis shows that Kant's thinking about labour, slavery, citizenship, the family, and sex developed in interlinked ways over several decades, culminating in his development of a 'new phenomenon in the juridical heavens', a 'trichotomy' of Right that thinks beyond the public/private divide by insisting upon a third sphere, organized by 'the right to a person akin to the right to a thing' (MM 6: 276; RDL 20: 460). This third dimension of Private Right is explicitly developed as a response to Kant's thinking about both sex and slavery, grounding his claim that slavery is inconsistent with right. Because work on Kant's account of slavery generally focuses on his arguments about race and colonialism, while his account of domestic right focuses on marriage, sex, and gender, the links between these arguments have been under-examined. But Kant himself understood the trich-otomy framework as a critical innovation in juridical philosophy, which shaped not only his understanding of domestic and slave labour, but also his famous distinction between active and passive citizenship, as well as the limits of public reason and civil equality.

Kant's theory of labour provides a vantage point for revealing the *structural* intersections of racism and sexism in his political thought, taking up the challenge Dilek Huseyinzadegan lays out in her 'For What Can the Kantian Feminist Hope?' (2018) by examining the continuities 'between our problems and Kant's' (10). In Kant's theory of labour, I find both complicity with emergent global patterns of patriarchy, white supremacy, and capitalism, as well as innovative theorizations of these problems that may offer critical resources to contemporary intersectional and materialist feminist theorizing. This approach takes Kant's racist and sexist thinking as an integral part of his philosophical system but understands these dimensions of his thinking as instructive since, as Huseyinzadegan puts it, 'we all know these contradictions exemplified in Kant's work are in fact representative of the larger contradictions of our lives today and are not so easily undone' (16).

Kant's thinking about labour presents us with a set of contradictions we have not resolved: contradictions between, on the one hand, an egalitarian vision of independent citizens and meritocratic pathways by which workers (and, perhaps, women) may 'work their way up' to full political participation, and on the other, deeply ingrained practices of enclosed economic dependency that make caregiving and reproductive labour precarious and insecure, and that shape and perpetuate stark raced, gendered, classed, and global inequalities. Contemporary scholarship that seeks to address inequality by drawing on Kantian accounts of dependency, poverty, and redistributive justice, then, must carefully attend to these patterned exclusions in order to avoid repeating them, and existing Kantian frames that take up race/racism and gender/sexism *separately* (or at best, as analogous problems) must learn to resist reinscribing patterns of erasure that treat dependencies as single-axis problems, which allows for *personal*, rather than *structural*, remedies. Tracking this problem requires new strategies within Kant scholarship to think beyond single-axis frameworks of oppression.

Thus, the genealogy of this project reaches beyond Kant scholarship, orienting its attention to labour – and in particular, to caregiving and other unwaged labour – through materialist and intersectional feminisms, which have long engaged in analyses of labour to identify patterns of exploitation and entitlement in liberal and legal theory.[5] It draws on intersectional feminism and twenty-first century work on global migration and care chains in order to identify domestic and caregiving labour as a global political problem that refuses to be contained by the 'restraining walls' (MM 6: 248) of the household. And it recognizes this analysis as particularly trenchant in the wake of a global pandemic in which the absence of adequate juridical frameworks for conceptualizing domestic and caregiving labour has become readily apparent; as the line between 'essential' and exploitative labour has blurred, these conceptual gaps have shaped starkly gendered and raced impacts.

At the same time, my analysis will locate the limits of labour-based analysis, building on arguments from the Black radical tradition that challenge the categories of exploited and alienated labour for conceptualizing enslavement and global conquest, thinking beyond Marxist (and Lockean) frames. I read Kant's linked analyses of slavery, sex work, and domestic labour through these arguments in order to map the edges of Kant's account of labour, the places where labour slides beyond exploitation and into subjection, objectification, and fungibility. Kant's practical philosophy, I argue, is particularly instructive for identifying these slides, both because of his explicit embrace of these moves in his anthropological and historical work, and because of the ways his analysis of

---

[5] From, for example, the wages for housework movement to the contemporary domestic workers alliance, to Pauli Murray and Kimberlé Crenshaw's trenchant uses of labour discrimination practices to ground first 'Jane Crow' and then intersectionality, which I discuss in Section 7.

labour does not exhaust the strategies available for addressing these slides in his moral and political philosophy. In making this argument, I build on Charles Mills' insight (2017) that Kant's philosophical system provides normative resources that Marx's lacks, showing that Kant, likewise, provides us with resources for theorizing unwaged labour that go beyond what we inherit from Marx (Pascoe 2017).

Thus, I argue neither that a labour analysis is sufficient for addressing normative inequality in Kant's practical philosophy, nor that it is sufficient for theorizing historical or contemporary practices of enslavement, extraction, or exploitation. Rather, I show that Kant's theory of labour sheds light on the normative structures of inequality built into his philosophy of Right, with implications for modern liberal frames that inherit from Kant. Kant's theorization of inequality takes race- and gender-based divisions of labour to be intertwined and mutually constitutive, revealing the ways that Kant's theorization of justice is explicitly white and male, organized against a raced and gendered backdrop of 'dependency' that places the labour of women, of non-whites, and in particular, of non-white women, outside the frame of justice.

This genealogy requires me to ask what it would mean not only to make Kant *useful* to feminist, decolonial, radical Black, and intersectional theorizing, but also to hold Kant *accountable* to these modes of theorizing. This means, as Patricia Hill Collins has put it, 'invoking concrete experience as a criterion of meaning' (1989: 769). Kant's thinking about the contradictions of labour are grounded in his own experiences, first as a tutor working within another's household, and later as a professor who employed a manservant of his own. Perhaps for this reason, his theorizing of labour is nuanced in ways that his thinking on race, gender, and sex often is not. But his thinking about labour cannot, and should not, be estranged from his prolific thinking about race, gender, sex, and class: holding Kant *accountable* to contemporary theorizing about race, gender, sex, and class means refusing to excise his practical philosophy from his anthropological, historical, and geographical work. While I treat the *Rechtslehre* as the final form of Kant's political philosophy, I explore *how* Kant arrived at these arguments through his long interrogation of the institutions that make moral life possible, which were informed and filtered through the development of his social theory and his engagement in contemporary debate. In doing so, I resist interpretive practices that compel me to read Kant as if his account of independence and public reason necessarily applied to me by, for example, setting aside his remarks about gender. In this, I am oriented by Tiffany Lethabo King's articulation of the training we are given as philosophers to identify *with* canonical figures like Kant, to locate ourselves in the text, and to offer slight adjustments that put ourselves – whether one is a woman, is Black, is Indigenous – at the centre of the text, as if the relevant mechanisms for 'working one's way up' applied to us (King 2017: 172). Rather, I want to think against and press on this training by refusing to acquiesce to the desire to find my own liberation in Kant's theory of freedom, attending instead to the structure and limits of Kantian independence. Reading Kant in this way, I will show, requires us to attend to the ways that his social theory is embedded in his account of Right.

I make this argument in seven moves. In Section 2, I develop Kant's theory of labour in the *Doctrine of Right* in order to examine the role labour plays in the patterns of exclusion built into the Kantian state. In Section 3, I turn to Kant's defence of the 'trichotomy' of Right in the drafts and Appendix of the *Doctrine of Right,* illuminating this argument as a critical and innovative feature of his political thought (VMM 20: 451). In Section 4, I explore Kant's early notes on political philosophy in order to map the development of his arguments about slavery and sex, which lead him to the framework of 'the right to a person akin to the right to a thing'. I argue that the linkage between marriage and slavery in these notes suggests that Kant's rejection of slavery in the *Doctrine of Right* may have as much to do with his theory of labour as it does with his changing thoughts on race. In Section 5, I explore the relationship between Kant's political theorization of labour and his anthropological accounts of race and gender, tracing a taxonomy of his thinking about labour, laziness, and leisure that reveals how his account of labour is consistent and continuous with his anthropological arguments and how, for Kant, gender is always raced. In Section 6, I examine the limits of Kant's account of labour, showing how sex work and slavery are critical exceptions to his account of enclosed domestic labour. I consider Kant's arguments about slavery and servitude in light of the politics of the historical process of emancipation and Reconstruction, showing how Kant's theory of labour maps strategies for embedding ongoing relations of racialized dependent labour after the abolition of slavery. In Section 7, I argue that Kant's theory of labour, with its nuanced and innovative account of domestic labour, provides a starting point for intersectional interrogations of Kantian philosophy that disrupt practices of theorizing about race and/or gender within Kant scholarship in ways that render women of colour invisible. In the concluding section, I argue that Kant's theory of labour disrupts moves that distinguish between Kant's systemic account of justice and his non-systemic discussions of domination and oppression, by showing how rightful (raced and gendered) inequality is embedded in his theory of the state.

2 Kant's Theory of Labour

Kant's interest in economics, from his emphasis on cosmopolitan trade to his study of Adam Smith, is apparent not just in his political and historical writings, but in moral texts like the *Groundwork*, where a Smithian division of labour frames the distinction between rational and empirical philosophy (GMS 4: 388), and the concept of *market price* is introduced to refine his definition of dignity (GMS 4: 434; Maliks 2014: 109; Fleischacker 1991). The market and its regulation were more than metaphors: economic realities and the institutions that organize everyday life were critical elements of Kant's empirical accounts of how juridical law and social context shape freedom (Fleischaker 1996; Flickshuh 2002). Thus, recent scholarship has foregrounded Kant's interest in economics and trade, examining Kantian economic justice within the state, from poverty relief to the state's duty to 'secure each person's right to access and participate in the public marketplace on equal terms' regardless of the economic system in place (Varden 2008: 342), as well as the role of global trade in Kant's cosmopolitanism.[6] Kant scholarship has also addressed labour, examining how employment contracts are needed to prevent us from using one another as a mere means (O'Neill 1989), exploring how Kant's theory of justice can counter the problems of exploitation (Wood 2017) and domination (Ripstein 2010), and exposing the role labour plays in Kant's account of citizenship (Pascoe 2015; Shell 2016; Hasan 2018; Basevich 2020; Moran 2021), his account of property acquisition (Ripstein 2010; Kirkland Forthcoming), and his account of contracts (Byrd 2002; Pallikkathayil 2010). My arguments in this section build upon this scholarship in order to develop a comprehensive account of the final form of Kant's theory of labour in the *Doctrine of Right*.

Kant's theory of labour is located at the intersection of innate and acquired right. Innate right is the right to humanity in our own person, expressed as freedom and innate equality. Kant describes it as the 'original right' to 'being one's own master', by which he means 'independence from being bound to others to more than one can in turn bind them' (MM 6: 237–8). Right (*Recht*) is repetitive the 'sum of the conditions' under which our reciprocal rights to this independence can be protected 'in accordance with a universal law of freedom' (MM 6: 230). Innate right, then, poses three puzzles for a Kantian account of labour. First, labour arrangements must respect the innate equality of employers

---

[6] For recent examinations of Kant's views on poverty relief and economic justice, see Allais 2015, Hasan 2018, Holtman 2018, Kleingeld 2014a, 2014b, Loriaux 2020, Sanchez Madrid 2018, Varden 2006b and 2020. I address Kant's arguments about poverty relief in Section 6.

and labourers; second, labour relations must be consistent with the right of each to be 'his own master'; third, labour contracts must respect our rights to our bodies as the means through which we set and pursue ends in the world, which means that we cannot enter into contracts to rent out our bodies. Kant's theory of labour must show that we can contract out our *labour*, while retaining rights to our *person*.

Kant solves these problems by theorizing labour relations as features of acquired right, which delineates relationships to things and persons, mapped through the institutions of Private Right. While Kant argues that labour is not a question of property right, since a person 'cannot be the owner of himself (*sui dominus*) (cannot dispose of himself as he pleases) – still less can he dispose of others as he pleases' (MM 6: 270), one's right to own the product of one's labour plays a key role in Kant's theory of labour, along with contracts (rights *against* specific persons) and domestic or status relations (rights *to* persons akin to our rights to things). As a question of acquired right, Kant's account of labour goes beyond questions of innate freedom and equality to consider the material conditions and relations of independence, as well as their implications for one's standing as a citizen in Public Right.

Kant's most straightforward analysis of labour is found in his account of contract right. Employment contracts are delineated in his 'Dogmatic Division of All Rights That Can Be Acquired by Contract'. Here, he recognizes three kinds of contracts to let and hire: contracts to lease or lend an object or property; contracts of 'letting work on hire' or labour contracts; and contracts 'empowering an agent' (MM 6: 285). All three are onerous contracts, in which each party acquires rights against the other.[7] The logic of letting and hiring labour is closely tied to that of letting and hiring objects, despite Kant's insistence that one's labour is not an object over which one can dispose. The 'letting work on hire' contract corresponds to a contract in which I hire someone to work in my factory or shop – a working day arrangement – while the 'empowering an agent' contract is a managerial contract, in which I contract to hire someone to manage my factory or shop to my specifications (Byrd 2002). In the first case, I contract for your labour, paying you a wage for your time or your product in a relation akin to Marx's conception of labour-value. In the second case, I contract for your full faculties to fulfil a limited set of

---

[7] These rights are framed as *specific*, although Onora O'Neill, in her account of Kantian employment contracts (1989), points out that employment contracts tend, in practice, to establish fairness by generalizing rather than establishing specific or individual contracts.

my ends, as determined by our employment contract. In the latter case, I may pay you an honorarium or salary as opposed to a wage.[8]

Contracts to let and hire, or to empower an agent, are consistent with innate equality because they are organized by a united will, which treats contracting parties *as if* they were equal in laying out the terms of the contract (even if the contract lays out a hierarchical relationship) (MM 6: 271).[9] And, they are consistent with my right to humanity in my own person, including my right to be 'my own master' in that what I rent out, in either case, is my labour, skill, or faculties, rather than my *person*. To make this distinction clear, Kant (and his critics) point to sex work and slavery (see Section 3) in order to make clear that we cannot rent out our person.

Kant develops his account of labour to ensure that rightful labour relations are consistent with innate right, but he concedes that some of these labour relations produce relations of dependency with political consequences. In his discussion of Public Right, Kant argues that the three requirements of citizenship are lawful freedom, civil equality, and civil independence. The first two derive from innate right: from one's right to be one's own master and not be bound by another in ways one could not reciprocally bind that other. But civil independence concerns acquired right and the material conditions of existence and preservation, or the attribute of 'owing his existence and preservation to his own rights and powers as a member of the commonwealth, not to the choice of another among the people' (MM 6: 314). Civil independence determines civil personality, or the right to represent oneself and participate in politics as an active citizen; passive citizens are those who have innate freedom and civil equality but lack civil independence.

The justification for this distinction was a pragmatic one that borrowed from the Abbe Sieyès' interpretation of Rousseau, which sought to establish a model of direct democracy in which voting rights were limited to property owners and taxpayers (Maliks 2014: 83–5). Kant's treatment of the distinction diverges from the French discourse in several ways: while Sieyès limited active citizenship to the 'third estate' in order to limit the power not only of the peasants, but of the

---

[8] Kant teases out the distinction in the *Feyerabend Lectures* (1784), where he distinguishes between wage labour, through which 'I grant another the use of my powers for a determined price' (Fey 27: 1361) so that my employer can 'determine the labour and can coerce it' (Fey 27: 1362), and an honorarium, 'which one of course cannot coerce' since it describes payment for a contract empowering another to act on my behalf, or on behalf of an institution, such as a professor, lawyer, or tutor (Fey 27: 1363). These examples suggest that the 'contract empowering an agent' category includes not just managerial contracts, but a wider range of contracts that organize others' rights to represent my interests, including lawyers, estate agents, doctors, and so on.

[9] I develop a full account of this argument in Pascoe 2013 (199), where I argue that because such contracts are designed to manage inequality, employees and employers are equal *in relation to the contract*, even if the contract sets out a relationship of inequality.

nobility and the clergy, Kant tied it to civil independence. This was, in part, motivated by a concern that those who owe their livelihoods to others could not be trusted to vote independently (Williams 2006) and could not reliably outsource their labour in order to participate in public affairs (Moran 2021). In making this distinction, Kant reconfigured the property requirement that had predominated since Locke,[10] arguing in *Theory and Practice* that an active citizen must be

> '*one's own master* (*sui iuris*), and thus that one has some *property* (which also includes any skill, trade, fine art, or science) that provides for one. That is to say that in those cases where he must earn his livelihood from others, he earns it only by *selling* what is *his*, not by means of granting others the right to make use of his powers, thus that he not *serve* anyone, in the true sense of the word, but the commonwealth' (TP 8: 295).[11]

By redefining 'property' to include a skill or a trade, Kant's distinction between active and passive citizenship turned primarily on labour relations, and thus, on one's location in market relations (Maliks 2014: 109).

Kant deploys a range of examples to illustrate the distinction, although he admits that it is 'somewhat difficult to determine the requirement for laying claim to the class in which one is one's own master' (TP 8: 295 n). The hairdresser who cuts my hair is dependent, while the wigmaker, who sells me a wig, is independent; the woodcutter who cuts my wood sells me his labour, while the tailor who transforms my fabric into clothing sells me his skill in the form of a final product. The wigmaker and the tailor would own the wig or the suit if I failed to pay them for it, and so what they sell me is the *product*, not their labour; they enter into a contract with me for trade, not for the use of their powers (TP 8: 295 n; MM 6: 314). In the *Doctrine of Right*, Kant emphasizes that this distinction is dependent on socio-economic context: a blacksmith in India 'who goes into people's houses to work on iron with his hammer, anvil, and bellows' is dependent, while the European blacksmith 'who can put the products of his work up as goods for sale to the public' is independent (MM 6: 314).

---

[10] Kant likewise rejects the Lockean argument that one's labour transforms one's right to property, explicitly arguing that 'working, enclosing, or in general transforming a piece of land can furnish no title of acquisition to it . . . whoever expends his labour on land that was not already his lost his pains and toil to who was first' (MM 6: 268–9). See Sections 5 and 6 for further discussion of Locke.

[11] Kant's account of active and passive citizenship evolved between the early drafts for *Theory and Practice* (1792–3) and its final form in his *Doctrine of Right* (1797). In the early drafts, Kant argued that 'the independence that is required to be a citizen of the state is the rightful condition of not standing under another's orders' (VTP Stark 245) so that 'a citizen is a human being in society who has his own rightful independence, i.e., can be considered as himself a member of the universal public legislative authority' (VTP 23: 137). Rafeeq Hasan has argued that Kant develops a more sophisticated and egalitarian account of the distinction in the *Doctrine of Right* (Hasan 2018: 925).

Labour is at the heart of Kant's account of civil independence in the *Doctrine of Right*, where citizenship is configured through the distinction between *independent labour*, in which one sells the *product* of one's labour and retains civil independence, and *dependent labour*, in which one rents out one's labour through either wage labour or managerial contracts, making one a dependent labourer and, thus, a passive citizen.[12] This has, as Rafeeq Hasan (2018) and Kate Moran (2021) have convincingly argued, more to do with structural features of the labour market than with wealth or property: the European blacksmith can access the raw materials of his trade without entering into contracts producing dependency, while the Indian blacksmith cannot. Likewise, we can imagine a wigmaker who is independent and yet struggles to keep her business running, while a wealthy athlete who owns property remains tied by a contract to dependency on his franchise (Moran 2021). Thus it is labour, rather than property alone, that determines civil independence: a labourer who owned his own home might yet be dependent because of the conditions of his labour.[13]

Because the citizenship distinction attends to the material conditions of civil independence, Kant insists that the distinction between active and passive citizenship is rightful because 'this dependence on the will of others and this inequality is, however, in no way opposed to their freedom and equality *as human beings*' (MM 6: 315). Civil independence justifies political inequality. But this political inequality is made consistent with innate right by a requirement of civil equality, namely, that 'it follows that, whatever sort of positive laws the citizens might vote for, these laws must still not be contrary to the natural laws of freedom and of the equality of everyone in the people corresponding to this freedom, namely, that anyone can work his way up from this passive condition to an active one' (MM 6: 315). This right 'to work his way up' to civil independence is a requirement of civil equality, which marks passive citizenship as a transitional state consistent with innate right, or our 'equality as human beings'.[14]

---

[12] Not all contracts empowering an agent produce dependence, as Kant notes in the *Feyerabend* lectures: while the manager of my factory is dependent upon me, the lawyer or doctor I pay (who may have other clients) is not dependent upon me in the same way: as an expert who is paid for his qualifications and skill, the standing of the lawyer or doctor is more akin to that of an independent labourer, even though our contract may take the form of empowering him as an agent to represent my interests in certain contexts. In the *Feyerabend*, Kant notes that contracts empowering an agent that do not produce dependency are paid through honoraria, rather than wages (Fey 27: 1363).

[13] Kant makes a similar point in rough notes for *Theory and Practice*, where he troubled the reliance on property ownership for determining citizenship, noting that those who own land but use it only for subsistence farming 'are not citizens of the state' because they 'do not contribute to the commonwealth' (VTP 23: 137).

[14] We see a variation of this argument in his account of marriage, where he squares the 'natural equality' of the married couple with the 'natural superiority of the husband to the wife' (MM 6: 279). The husband's superiority, moreover, is not merely 'natural'; it is institutionally organized,

The 'anyone can work his way up' requirement has yielded significant debate within Kantian scholarship about *who* can work their way up, and under what conditions. Kant's citizenship hierarchy maps rightful class distinctions organized through labour rather than hereditary privilege, marking a historical transition from an aristocratic to a 'meritocratic' account of class relations.[15] But as feminist Kantians have persistently pointed out, Kant's account of dependence is not merely classed, but gendered.[16] Kant's initial definition of active citizenship, in the drafts for *Theory and Practice*, is explicit about these limits, claiming that independence hinges upon being 'not wife, child, and household servant' and defining access to wives, children, and household servants as 'the set of capacities which makes this independence possible' which pertains to 'one who, regarding his subsistence, has within himself a part of the state's powers that rest upon his free choice (a household)' (VTP Stark: 245). Civil independence, then, is gendered – an argument elaborated in Kant's infamous claim that only men can qualify as active citizens, whether because this is a 'natural' requirement, as he argues in *Theory and Practice*, or because 'all women' depend, for their preservation, on 'arrangements made by another' (MM 6: 314). Kantians have debated whether this argument reflects Kant's intractable 'woman problem' (Cash 2002; Maliks 2014; Mendus 1992) or a highly gendered institutional order in which wives are dependent on husbands (Sabourin 2021; Williams 2006). These arguments suggests that while class distinctions might be rightful (as long as one can 'work his way up'), when these distinctions turn on a permanent feature of one's identity (gender and, as we will see, race) then they would seem to violate basic Kantian principles of equality and innate right. So, a 'better Kantianism' must be committed to the premise that anyone, women included, can work their way up (Varden 2006b; Weinrib 2008). But this move is troubled, I will argue in the remainder of this section, by distinctions *within* Kant's account of dependent labour that provide us with crucial resources for understanding both Kant's theory of the state, and the emergence of the bourgeois household at the end of the eighteenth century.

---

through his ability to determine and promote the ends of the household – ends which, as we will see, he sets and she shares. Insofar as this project of sharing ends is cooperative, the husband is the wife's 'superior' but not her 'master'; she is dependent on him (and thus, lacks civil personality) but she nevertheless retains, thanks to innate right, her lawful freedom and civil equality; it is this very lawful freedom and civil equality that allows her to enter into a relationship characterized by shared ends.

[15] In the *Doctrine of Right*, Kant notes that 'conferring hereditary privilege' is 'contrary to right' (MM 6: 329) and replaces a hereditary class hierarchy with a class hierarchy based in labour distinctions. For a discussion of how Kant's arguments responded to contemporary debates about class and hereditary privilege, see my 'A Universal Estate?' (2018).

[16] In Sections 5, 6, and 7, I show that it is also raced.

Kant's account of labour is central to his theory of the state because it determines access to political participation. This was a problem that Kant had engaged with long before landing on the active/passive citizenship distinction – namely, in his account of the public uses of reason in his 1784 essay *What Is Enlightenment*. There, Kant's claim that that 'the entire fair sex' lacks the courage to emerge from 'self-incurred immaturity' and to 'use one's own understanding without the guidance of another' (WIE 8: 35) is grounded in an account of dependency echoed in the citizenship argument. Charlotte Sabourin has argued that Kant's argument hinges on at least two conceptions of immaturity: immaturity in the sense of uncritical uses of reason, and immaturity in the sense of dependency, or those who lack civil maturity (2021). The former might correspond to the 'natural' justification for women's exclusion that we find in *Theory and Practice*, and the latter to the dependency clause he emphasizes in *The Doctrine of Right*. Whether women's immaturity is natural or institutionally enforced, the question remains: can women, like other dependent workers, work their way up to active political participation – or is women's dependency special?

The answer lies, I argue, in the role Kant's account of labour plays in his delineation of political participation. The distinction between public reason and citizenship is instructive here. The former names the right to speak in public, which is open to all citizens of the commonwealth provided that they speak *publicly*, which means independent of private office (WIE 8: 38), while the latter refers to institutionalized political participation (voting) which is, as Maliks points out, 'a zero sum game' (2014: 108): we can publicly dissent from a law or an institution even as we follow that law or fulfil our obligations to that institution, but our vote either supports or conflicts with those obligations. Thus, dependent citizens who are barred from voting may be able to participate in public reason, provided that they speak publicly, *as if* they were independent of their private offices and dependencies. Dependency alone, then, is not sufficient to explain women's exclusion from the public sphere, since Kant explicitly imagines instances in which those who serve an institution's or business's private interests have the right to publicly dissent from those interests. While Kant's primary example of this is the clergyman, it is also critical to a just account of labour relations. Because of their material dependence on their employers, contract labourers cannot vote, but it is consistent with Kant's account of public reason to imagine that they must be able to engage in the public use of reason in order to advocate for better working conditions, fairer labour contracts, and, one might imagine, the right to unionize.

The puzzle, then, is why women's material dependence blocks them from *both* the political participation of active citizens, *and* from participation in public reason. As many scholars have noted, the structure and domain of public reason is highly gendered, both in that the public sphere was historically constructed through the exclusion of women (Schott 1997) and because a 'new, austere style of public speech was promoted, a style deemed "rational," "virtuous," and "manly"' (Fraser 1990: 59). But we know, too, that women across Europe were actively resisting their exclusion from the public sphere and from the public use of reason, and that several of Kant's contemporaries, including his frequent dinner companion Theodor von Hippel, the mayor of Konigsberg, made impassioned arguments for women's inclusion in the public sphere, in the public use of reason, and in the right to vote (Pascoe 2018). Kant's reliance on the 'natural' exclusion of women would have been troubled by these arguments.

By distinguishing Kant's arguments about gender from his arguments about labour, many Kantian analyses of both the citizenship and the public reason arguments blur a crucial distinction in Kant's vision of the structure of the state. The key is a distinction *within* the category of dependent labour: a distinction between the dependence of 'rights against persons' and the dependence of 'rights to persons akin to rights to things'. In making this argument, I build on Kantian feminist scholarship that has emphasized the importance of the domestic sphere in Kant's political philosophy, identifying it as an essential feature of the just state, organizing intimate household relationships including parenthood and caregiving, marriage and sex, and servitude and domestic labour (Herman 1993; Schapiro 1999; Varden 2018). The parent–child relation is an instructive example for delineating the distinct logic of the domestic sphere and its role in shaping access to political participation, since we are accustomed to thinking of children as 'passive' citizens and to assuming, as Kant suggests, that children will have the opportunity, upon their majority, to 'work their way up' to full citizenship (MM 6: 267).[17] In order to ensure that parents do not merely treat their children as means to their own ends, this relation must be authorized and enforced through 'the right to a person akin to the right to a thing', or the distinctive structure of right that Kant attributes to the domestic sphere.[18]

---

[17] For nuanced discussions of the rights of children in Kant's *Doctrine of Right,* see Schapiro (1999) and Varden (2012).

[18] I will refer to 'the right to a person akin to the right to a thing' as *domestic right* as opposed to *status rights*, both because Kant himself referred to these rights as 'domestic' and in order to clarify the scope and location of this form of right in light of the varied definitions of status rights in contemporary Kantian scholarship. My understanding of domestic right hews closer to Helga Varden's map of status rights that 'concern holding between spouses, between families and their servants and between parents and their children' (2012: 335) than Arthur Ripstein's broader definition, which takes status rights to include examples such as parent–child relations, teacher–student relations, legal relations between fiduciaries and beneficiaries, and employment relations more generally (2010: 70–7). Ripstein's status relations include but are not limited to relations within the domestic sphere; they include employment contracts and contracts empowering

But when we take the parent–child relation as paradigmatic of domestic right, we miss two structural elements of Kant's account of equality, independence, and labour. First, attending to the parent–child relationship emphasizes the role of the state in supporting dependency relations while mapping those relations as temporary and thus, as consistent with civil equality. Other relations of dependence within the domestic sphere – namely, those of wives and servants – are *structurally* permanent, insofar as the domestic realm is premised upon their labour. Second, we miss the degree to which the dependence of wives and servants – unlike the dependence of children – is a form of dependent *labour*, organized not through contract but through 'the right to a person akin to the right to a thing'.[19] In the parent–child relation, the child's dependence necessitates the parent's labour. The inverse is true for the wife and the servant, who perform the bulk of domestic labour for the husband/head of household: their dependence necessitates their labour. These, then, are not merely relations of dependence, but of dependent labour.

When we parse domestic right as a distinct set of labour practices within Kant's account of Private Right, we find that Kant has offered us a framework for distinguishing labour within the household and outside it, which is critical to understanding the structure of civil independence, citizenship, and civil equality's 'work one's way up' requirement. With this distinction in hand, we can clarify how the passivity of wives (and servants) is distinct from the passivity of workers so that a *gendered divisions of labour*, rather than merely gender *itself*, organizes civil equality and access to civil independence. As I will show in the next section, this analysis of domestic labour can solve the dependency riddle in Kant's account of citizenship and the public sphere, with important implications for the structure of the rightful state itself.

3 'A New Star': Kant's 'Trichotomy' Argument

In a review written shortly after the publication of the *Doctrine of Right* in February 1797, Friedrich Bouterwek remarks that 'our jurists and philosophers will be surprised by this, but Mr. Kant contends there is actually a third, namely a *personal* right as a thing. What this is, or is supposed to be, will surprise many even more than the new idea itself' (RDL 20: 448). The innovative new right Bouterwek remarks upon is, of course, the 'right to a person akin to the right to

---

agents 'in which one person makes arrangements for another' (2010: 76); this frame, unlike domestic rights, does not distinguish between the case of wives and servants on the one hand, and contractual employment or agential relations on the other.

[19] Kant is clear that parents have a duty to support the development of minor children (MM 6: 360), while children have no duties to work for their parents, owing them, at best, 'a duty of gratitude' (MM 6: 281).

a thing', or the structure of Right that organizes the domestic sphere. While relatively little attention has been paid to this third part of Kant's Private Right in contemporary scholarship beyond the robust discussion of Kant's theory of marriage inaugurated by Herman's article, it was recognized as a key innovation not only by Kant's critics, but by Kant himself. In response to Bouterwek's review, Kant added an Appendix to the *Doctrine of Right* where he elaborated on this third form of right, calling it 'a new phenomenon in the juristic sky' and reflecting on its historical emergence, asking whether it is 'a *stella mirabilis* (a phenomenon never seen before, growing into a star of the first magnitude but gradually disappearing again, perhaps to return at some time) or merely a *shooting star*' (MM 6: 358–9).

The Appendix offers an extended discussion of the necessity of the new domain of Private Right, noting that the dichotomy of rights to things and rights against persons 'might also be a fourfold division' incorporating both the 'right to a thing akin to a right against a person' and a 'right to a person akin to the right to a thing' (MM 6: 358). The former 'drops out without further ado, since to right of a thing against a person is inconceivable' but the latter 'belongs necessarily (as given *a priori* in reason) to the concept of what is externally mine or yours' (MM 6: 358). In the draft for this section, Kant repeatedly refers to the necessity of the right to a person akin to the right to a thing as forming a 'trichotomy' in the system of the concept of rights (RDL 20: 451,460): a distinction between property, contract, and domestic rights. Attending to this 'trichotomy' argument, I will argue, allows us to make sense of the distinct forms of labour, dependency, and erasure that organize Kant's account of citizenship and the public sphere, while at the same time recognizing Kant's innovative account of the emerging bourgeois household.

The 'right to a person akin to the right to a thing' reframes relations within the household in terms of *possession*: while an employer has rights *against* those he employs through contract, a householder has rights *to* his wife, children, and servants, though these rights *to* are, like all property rights, really rights *against* everyone else. The 'possession' in question, then, is *intelligible* possession: a householder 'acquires' a wife in that it would be 'a wrong (an infringement on my freedom which can coexist with the freedom of everyone in a universal law) to prevent me from using [her] as I please; (MM 6: 249). Domestic relationships are by definition *exclusive*: marriage must be (for Kant) monogamous, parents have special duties to care for their own children, and household employers may 'retrieve' servants who run away, thanks to their special right 'to' them (MM 6: 283).

While domestic relationships like marriage and servitude are constituted through contract, domestic contracts are importantly different from other labour contracts, in that they are not just a contract to *let and hire (location conductio operae)* but a giving up of their persons into the possession of the head of the house, a lease (*location conductio personae*). What distinguishes such a contract from letting and hiring is that the servant agrees to *do whatever is permissible* for the welfare of the household, instead of being commissioned for a specifically determined job, whereas someone who is hired for a specific job (an artisan or a day labourer) does not give himself up as part of the other's belongings and so is not a member of the household (MM 6: 361).

Domestic contracts produce not a right against a person, but a relation of exclusive possession. While a waged employee might deploy public reason in the public sphere *as if* he were independent, the domestic servant, the wife, and the child are *exclusively* dependent on the master/husband/father; there is no way to treat them *as if* they were not. The wage labourer – even the day labourer or artisan who does a job within a domestic space – has agreed only to the specifications of a contract, to a given amount of work to fulfil the employer's stated ends. The domestic servant (or wife), on the other hand, has agreed to take the household's ends as his (or her) own;[20] the domestic labour contract delineates one's relationship to the ends of the household, rather than specifying the kind or amount of labour this will require. This explains Kant's uncompromising exclusion of wives, children, and servants from the public sphere.

Examining domestic right as a set of labour relations, then, allows us to clarify distinctions between wage labour and domestic labour that are blurred in general analyses of dependency. Wage labour contracts are organized, as we have seen, so that employers gain rights *against* their employees for a particular set of deeds (be it hours of work or items produced), while employees gain rights *against* their employers for pay; this contract aligns a particular set of ends for the employer and employee, ensuring that they can each pursue their ends (be it production or pay) through a right to the other's deed. Domestic labour contracts, on the other hand, involve an open-ended agreement to 'do whatever is necessary for the welfare of the household' as determined by a shared set of ends (MM 6: 283). To say that household ends are *shared* is to say that each party's ends are *transformed by* their agreement to share ends within the household: they come into *possession* of one another's ends. This is importantly different from contractual agreements, which *align* rather than *transforming* ends. Thus, there is no sense in which the domestic servant (or wife) can behave *as if* she is independent of the householder, since she has

---

[20] In an early set of notes from 1769, Kant introduces the distinction between domestic and public servants, arguing that 'a servant is one who sees to the *personal comfort* of another at his command. An assistant for his business. An officer sees to the *public business* at the command of another' (J 19: 472, unpublished translation). Thus, unlike public servants, domestic servants are asymmetrically dependent upon their master precisely because these ends are *private*.

adopted these ends *as her own*. This is the answer to the dependency riddle above: domestic relations, including contracts for domestic labour, establish a relation of dependency that precludes access to the public sphere. This is an *enclosed* dependence, organized through shared ends so that dependents cannot behave *as if* they are independent.

If the household is organized by a duty to share ends, then who sets these ends? Kant is explicit, in both his political and anthropological arguments, about the asymmetries of household relations, describing the household as a 'society of unequals' (MM 6: 283): wives and domestic servants take household ends set by the husband or householder (MM 6: 279) as their own, just as the householder takes the 'feeding and protection' of the wife, child, and servant as his end. Kant's claim that 'woman should *dominate* and the man should *govern*' (Anth 7: 309) and his description of the 'natural superiority of the husband to the wife in his capacity to promote the common interest of the household' (MM 6: 279) make clear that the husband sets ends which wives and servants must not only share, but pursue, following orders for 'whatever is necessary for the good of the household' (MM 6: 283). Thus, while the husband or householder sets these ends, it is often up to the wife and servants to determine what reproductive or caregiving labour is necessary for the good of the household. In this sense, as Charlotte Sabourin notes, the householder may find himself dependent upon his wife or his servant in domestic matters, but while a wife may be 'mature' in her dealings with household affairs, she is still judged immature in the context of enlightenment (2021: 245); her husband remains 'her natural curator' (Anth 7: 209) and 'this legal immaturity with respect to public transactions makes woman all the more powerful in respect to domestic welfare' (Anth 7: 209).[21] While Kant nods to the 'immaturity' of the householder in domestic matters, his reliance on both this labour and its attendant use of reason is not mapped as a form of dependence in Kant's conception of citizenship; rather, it is proof of and the condition for the possibility of his independence.[22]

---

[21] Kant is even sharper in his assessment of the asymmetries of dependence on domestic servants, generalizing about them, in the notes for *Theory and Practice*, as 'a human being who, like a parasitic plant, is rooted only on another citizen' (VTP 23: 137).

[22] Access to domestic labour is necessary but not sufficient for independence; wage labourers may be dependent upon wives and servants without qualifying for civil independence. There are gestures in some of Kant's notes towards an awareness of dependency upon this labour. In notes on the *Observations*, Kant notes his dependence on the labour of craftsmen, saying 'Were I to enter the workshop of a craftsman, I would wish that he could not read my thoughts[.] I fear this comparison, [as] he would realise the vast inequality I find myself in with respect to him. I see well enough that I could not live one day without his industriousness, that his children are raised to be useful people' (AA RDL 20: 102). With thanks to Corey Dyck for the translation.

This is not to say, of course, that those in conditions of domestic dependency could not 'work their way up' as Kant's account of citizenship suggests: children are dependants who may become independent upon their majority if they meet the requirements for doing so. We can imagine, as feminist Kantians often do, that women may work their way up by becoming householders or obtaining positions that otherwise make them independent. But this argument often takes relations within the household to be organized through *personal* dependency, rather than *structural* dependency (Pascoe 2015; Hasan 2018). Kant's reliance on dependent labour to structure the distinction between active and passive citizenship ensures that while it may be the case that *anyone* can work his way up, it is not possible for *everyone* to work their way up, since *someone* will have to do dependent labour. A given factory worker may open a textile shop and become an active citizen, but someone else will take her place in the factory; as women work outside the household as professors, lawyers, wigmakers, and public servants, they outsource domestic and reproductive labour to others who thereby become dependent (Pascoe 2015).[23] Kant himself predicted this outsourcing, arguing that the non-sexual labours of the household may be outsourced to servants 'if the husband is rich enough' so that the wife is 'not to be troubled to assist with matters of domestic well-being' (Anth-Frie 20: 465).

I return to this question of outsourcing in Section 7; for now, it is enough to note that the contracts that organize wage labour and domestic labour play a critical role in making relations of dependency *rightful*: as Ripstein puts it, 'cooperation contrasts with domination when it is voluntary on both sides' (2010: 47). If domestic labour is voluntary – so that, alternatively, one could simply 'work one's way up' – then the enclosed dependence of the domestic sphere is consistent with civil equality. But if this right to 'work one's way up' is premised upon patterns of outsourcing, the coercive background conditions that ensure access to reproductive labour become more difficult to ignore. And, when we examine these patterns of outsourcing with an eye on how Kant's thinking about gender (and race) informs his analysis of labour and dependence, they become a problem for Kantian theories of justice.

These patterns are central to Kant's account of civil independence, although they remain invisible when we ignore the *material conditions* of this independence.

---

[23] Reinar Maliks observes that Kant, like Smith, may have hoped that the growth of the market sphere might have the effect of discouraging reliance on domestic servitude, encouraging householders to spend money on market services rather than on servants (2014: 109), but as I have argued elsewhere, the contemporary economy continues to treat reproductive and caregiving labour as a form of 'a right to a person akin to the right to a thing' organized by informal and unenforceable agreements distinct from the kinds of labour contracts that operate in other spheres (see Pascoe 2015).

When we do so, Kant's own reliance on his manservant, Lampe, for the daily reproduction that made his labour as a scholar and citizen possible is out of the frame, and Lampe's total dependence upon Kant, in accordance with this 'most personal of rights' ensures that this dependence remains invisible in Kant's public life. But if this reproductive and domestic labour is out of the frame of Kant's public and political spheres, its place in his theory of right nevertheless carefully theorized in ways that are instructive. As I have argued elsewhere, the domestic sphere and reproductive labour are actually more rigorously theorized in Kant than in Marx, for whom domestic and caregiving labour is often visible only when it is disrupted or subsumed by capitalist labour relations (Pascoe 2017). Kant's innovative 'trichotomy' argument thus precedes Hegel's tripartite distinction between the political sphere, civil society, and the family, and grounds this distinction in a nuanced account of domestic right that is not captured in Hegel's reference to the 'contractual' basis of Kant's account of marriage. In its explicit theorization of the distinction between market and domestic labour, Kant's 'right to a person akin to the right to a thing' provides a crucial dimension missing in Marx's analyses of labour, identifying the economic role of household labour at a critical historical moment, as the bourgeois household coalesces as a necessary site of unwaged labour to support the reproduction of the burgeoning global capitalist market. In this sense, his 'trichotomy' argument is indeed 'a *stella mirabilis*', a 'new phenomenon in the juristic sky' (MM 6: 358).

We have seen that Kant's 'trichotomy' structure of right allows him to theorize not merely a distinction between 'public' and 'private', but between public, market, and domestic realms, each with its own labour logic which correspond to the trichotomy of property right, contract right, and domestic right. Those who *own* product of their labour – whether in the sense that they own the product, the means of production, or the skill, trade, or art in question – are *independent*, and so have full access to the public sphere. Those who grant others rights to their labour through contracts in the market sphere are *dependent*, and so their access to political participation is mediated by this dependence. They are dependent in that they do not own the product of their labour, but their employer has only rights *against* them (rather than rights *to* them). Their ends are their own, ensuring that they can still act *as if* they were independent for the purposes of public reason, and that they have the freedom to 'work their way up' to independence (though their capacity to work their way up does not transform the economic structure in which dependent labour is necessary). Those who agree to give another a right *to* their labour in the domestic sphere are characterized by *enclosed dependence*, through which they grant their employer (or husband) the right to use them as a person – which is to say, the right to their ends, as well as their agency in fulfilment of his ends, so long as he does not 'use them up' (MM 6: 283). This involves an agreement to take his ends as their own (not merely to act *as if* they were their own) and in return, to have their support (e.g., being 'fed and protected') as a *member* of the household be included in these ends. Thus, enclosed dependent labourers have no rights *against* their employers, only rights *to* the protection of their employers, which is to say that while the fact of their dependency is authorized by the state, the particular duties that constitute their dependence are subject to an agreement of shared ends, which are opaque from the perspective of law. Those who labour in this third sphere, therefore, cannot act *as if* they were independent, and are thus excluded from political participation.

Kant's trichotomy argument is a critical and underexamined feature of his political philosophy, which allows us to better understand both the structure of gender, and of the gendered division of labour, within his political thought. Focusing on the role of labour in domestic right unsettles familiar feminist treatments of Kant's account of 'the right to a person akin to the right to a thing', which have overwhelmingly focused on marriage. But feminists are right to point to the ways in which Kant develops this framework of right in order to grapple with thorny problems of sex and objectification: Kant's early notes reveal that 'the right to a person akin to the right to a thing' develops in response to persistent difficulties in theorizing rightful sexual relations. But, as I will show in the next section, sex was not the only problem this form of right was designed to solve: the 'trichotomy' framework emerges out of a set of questions about labour and its limits, in Kant's interlinked arguments about marriage, sex, servants, and slavery.

4 Of Sex and Slavery: The Development of Domestic Right

Kant's trichotomy argument, in which he distinguished between contract and domestic labour, was the culmination of a decades-long set of reflections on the organization of work. His account of the household as a domestic society comprised of marital, parental, and master–servant relations was inspired by Gottfried Achenwall's account in *Natural Law*, which served as the textbook for Kant's lectures on political philosophy in the 1770s and 1780s. Kant's notes on the textbook and for his lectures contend with several conceptual difficulties in relation to domestic life that inform his later development of domestic right and labour relations. For the purposes of this argument, I will focus on two: his interlinked arguments about marriage, slavery, and sex work, and his arguments about the distinction between servants and enslaved people or serfs.[24]

---

[24] Kant sometimes refers to serfs interchangeably with slaves (MM 6: 241), suggesting that he saw the conditions of serf and enslaved labour as analogous in being properly located beyond labour. I do not assume that Kant's references to slavery necessarily refer to Black chattel slavery in the New World, in light of arguments made by Inez Valdez (2020) and Huaping Lu-Adler (2022a),

The first argument is better known, thanks to feminist analyses of Kant's views on sex, marriage, and sex work. Kant returns repeatedly to the problem of sex work in order to map the limits of both contract right and domestic right. In the *Doctrine of Right*, he argues that sex work contracts cannot be valid (MM 6: 279), since sex involves the use of a person as a thing, and 'if one were make oneself such a thing by *contract*, the contract would be contrary to law' (MM 6: 360). The sex work case had troubled Kant for a long time, showing up in his lectures on ethics and politics, and in his drafts and notes. In the Collins lecture notes, for example, Kant notes that 'man can certainly enjoy the other as an instrument for his service; he can utilize the other's hands or feet to serve him, though by the latter's free choice' (Eth-Col 27: 384) but distinguishes these cases of enjoying a person as an 'instrument for his service' from that of enjoying the person as an object. Thus, when I hire a masseuse, it is their labour I rent; when I hire a sex worker, it is their *person* I rent, making them into an *object* in violation of innate right. Kant makes a key distinction here, between the potential use of the masseuse as a *means only* – a problem of exploitation remedied by contract, which aligns relevant ends – and the use of the sex worker *as a thing*. The problem of using a person *as a thing* is not remedied by aligning our ends through contract, and so contracts are *insufficient* for making sex work rightful.

This insufficiency long troubled Kant. In notes from his early (1769–70) reflections on political philosophy, Kant reveals a lack of certainty about the nature of sexual contracts, noting that 'it is not a question of whether prostitution and concubinage are morally possible, but whether they also can be contrary to right. Namely whether someone could acquire leasing or hiring, a right to intercourse or a deflowering' and concluding that 'I can not say, whether there is a right to dispose of parts of one's body' (J 19: 458 *Refl* 7570). In other words, when addressing the question through a consideration of contract right alone, Kant cannot answer it.

Thus, he begins to tease out the distinction between contract and property right with regards to sex, answering the question by noting 'on the contract in which someone disposes over his person for the use of the other[:] They are all null and void except matrimony; for no one is his own property because otherwise he is a thing insofar as he is disposed and insofar as he disposes is a person. If [someone] however can dispose over him, he can have no rights'

---

who have advanced complicated readings of the forms of slavery to which Kant attended. But we must also not assume Kant was not attentive to the Atlantic slave trade and forms of slavery within the Americas: we know that Kant carefully followed debates about the slave trade, and may have been influenced in his thinking on slavery by the unfolding revolution in Saint Domingue (Haiti) (Kleingeld 2014a; Valdez 2020); I explore this context in Section 5.

(J 19: 458 *Refl* 7572). Kant's first intervention is the rejection of the idea that we are our own property to be disposed of, which allows him to reject the possibility of sexual contracts. In a later note, he introduces marriage as the sole exception to this, since it involves 'ownership of what is used regarding the sexual organs' (J 19: 460, *Refl* 7580). Here, we see Kant rethinking sexual access as a question of property – a right *to* the sexual organs, rather than a right *against* the person in possession of them. Because sex is the use of a person *as a thing*, it is not a sort of labour for let and hire, but a question of possessive right.

Kant struggles to articulate the sort of right that this marital possession entails, arguing, 'this *dominum utile* cannot be separated from right to use. It is not divisible and it is not alienable. It is right in a thing. For it is right in the organ not to performance of service. Despite this there is no right in a thing extended to another person' (J 19: 460 *Refl* 7580). Our rights of sexual access, as he puts it in a later addendum to this note, 'can be gained by another only under condition of ownership': sexual access, in other words, can *only* be understood as a form of property right, rather than as a kind of labour. This reading squared with existing conceptions of domestic relations as primarily possessive, but the purely possessive frame for mapping domestic relations sat uncomfortably for Kant: these notes reveal the degree to which Kant found the existing formations of rights – namely, rights *to* things and rights *against* persons–inadequate for making sense of sexual use. He rejects the idea that I can have a right against a person for the performance of sexual services, since he understood sex to be a kind of *use*, rather than a kind of *labour.* But this didn't sit right either, since a right to *use* a part of a person treated one's sexual attributes as a kind of property.

The inadequacies of this framework were not limited to sex: Kant repeatedly relates the problem of sex to that of slavery. In Feyerabend's 1784 notes on Kant's political philosophy lectures, we see the two cases being equated. In notes on coercion, Feyerabend rehearses the argument against enforcing sex work contracts, following this with 'also if a human being sells himself into bondsmanship his contract is not valid. I am free, for that reason I cannot throw my freedom away. In relation to marriage, more will be said' (Fey 27: 1336). And indeed, in notes on the domestic sphere, he writes 'I can place myself into service by contract only for labour, it is a duty that no human being can dispose over his whole self. Is marriage thus also impossible? No, this is the single exception' (Fey 27: 1379). Kant's consideration of sex work provided him a framework to trouble the limits of contract labour and to examine the problem of slavery; repeatedly, he mentions marriage as the sole exception to this problem. The problem of slavery is akin to the problem of sex, since both are configured as cases where one uses a person *as a thing*, rather than merely as a means; the problem of sex and slavery is not one of exploitation, but of possession and use.

Kant's discussion of slavery is not limited to his discussion of sex; it is also tied to his notes on labour in the domestic sphere in the 1770s and 1780s, where he struggles to delineate slave labour from servitude, since both involve right to all works rather than letting for hire for specific work. Kant's notes on slavery in reference to the Achenwall textbook are of particular interest, given that Achenwall theorized explicitly about contemporary enslavement and the rights of slave owners, and had written, in other contexts, about slave law in the Americas.[25] Achenwall's account does not provide a clear distinction between slavery and servitude, in part because he does not object to slavery, and in part because he includes forced indentured servitude as a category that blurs the difference.

Kant's notes on these sections reveal that he found existing frameworks, of rights *to* or *against* persons, to be inadequate for teasing out this distinction (J 19: 557 *Refl* 7927). He suggests that the distinction rests upon the *permanence* of the relation, arguing in his lectures on Achenwall: 'a subject who is obligated to perform domestic labour for his keep is called *famulus* (a servant) . . . *famulus* can be obligated *as* to provide all his labours throughout his entire life or to particular labours during intervals. In the first case the *famulus* is *servus* (a slave) and *herus* is *dominus* (owner) but in the latter case he remains *famulus* (servant)' (Fey 27: 1380).[26] Service is distinguished from slavery, then, in that the servant has the right to cancel the contract while the slave does not.

These notes reveal the close linkages between Kant's conception of the dependency of slavery and that of domestic relations, and the inadequacies of existing frameworks for delineating permissible labour relations in the domestic sphere – and for developing definitive arguments against enslavement. Accordingly, Kant's consideration of slavery in his notes from the 1780s centre

---

[25] Achenwall published 'Observations on North America' (1767), drawn directly from Benjamin Franklin's testimony on a visit to Hanover in the 1760s, which reflected on North American and Caribbean slave practices, as well as indentured servitude. Admittedly, the Observations was written after the Natural Law textbook on which Kant relied, which was an edition from 1763, though they were widely republished in magazines throughout Prussia. The sections in Achenwall's textbook on slavery are quite detailed, including reference to manumission and freedmen, as well as to distinctions within slave contracts. See Juhnke (1974); Achenwall (2021).

[26] His notes on Achenwall make the same point: 'one can suspend but not renounce his freedom, for *usum virium suarum alteri* {the use of one's powers by another} can be conceded but not alienated. It is not *location operae* {letting for hire for specific work} to the other of a *jus in omnes operas* {right to all works}, also it would strike us as unbearable to give lifelong consent' (J 19: 557). This insight leads Kant to admit that, likewise, marital consent cannot be 'indissoluble' (J 19: 547).

on its permissibility, particularly as a form punishment for crimes (cf. Fey 27: 1381, 1335; J 19: 475, 547, 548, 557, 558, 559).

It is telling, then, that Kant clarifies his position on slavery not by distinguishing it from servitude, but by distinguishing it from marriage. In these early notes, marriage is the 'single exception' (Fey 27: 1379) to the impermissibility of contracts to make use of another person; such contracts, including slavery and sex work 'are all null and void except *matrimonium*' (J 19: 458 *Refl* 7572). It is in his reflections on marriage as a solution to the problem of sexual use that Kant first formulates the third domain of possessive right as a solution to the problem that, as he puts it in a note for his lectures on Achenwall, 'we can of course acquire the use of things but not of persons' (J 19: 543 *Refl* 7880). But Kant presents the solution in a footnote added in the 1780s: 'there ought to be a *jus in re* {right in a thing} and yet at the same time a *jus personale* {right in a person}, i.e., to the person alone and depending on her will. There must therefore be a right that extends not merely to a person regarding a particular use but to the entire will of the person, i.e., the entire person herself must be acquired' (J 19: 544, *Refl* 7880). This right, which would be developed into a right to a person akin to the right to a thing, transforms not only Kant's conception of marriage, but domestic labour and slavery as well. It allows him to show that household relations do not require wives and domestic servants to dispose of themselves as things, and therefore to definitively claim that those labour relations that *do* treat persons as things – namely, sex work and slavery – have no place in a scheme of right.[27]

This link between Kant's account of marriage and slavery allows us to complicate established narratives about Kant's conceptions of race and slavery. While Kant was justifying race-based slavery in his anthropology through the late 1780s, he was also grappling with critiques of slavery as a form of labour in his work on domestic labour and marriage, where he was developing the framework of 'the right to a person akin to the right to a thing' to organize marriage and domestic servitude in way that could be distinguished from both

---

[27] Kant's development of the 'right to a person akin to the right to a thing' as the most 'personal' of rights, distinct from a purely possessive right to persons, runs parallel to innovations in slave law during the same period. Roy Copeland (2010) has argued that throughout the eighteenth century, the legal standing of slaves as a form of real estate, personal chattel, or a hybrid was uncertain, but this question was settled in 1792 in Virginia, when the state legislature declared all slaves 'personal chattel' rather than real estate (950). As Copeland notes, the distinction made little difference in the lived experience of the enslaved, but it reflected the development of an increasingly sophisticated logic of slave law, as well as granting slave owners more freedoms to dispose of or rent out their slaves, by making their rights to slaves personal, rather than entailed to estates. By redefining slavery as a 'personal', rather than purely a property right, slave law from the 1790s onwards treated the dependency of slaves as akin to the dependency of wives under couverture, producing patterns of domestic dependency akin to those developed by Kant.

wage labour and slavery. This may offer an alternative explanation for Kant's apparent 'change of mind' about race in the final decade of his career (Kleingeld 2007, 2014a). Since Kant continued to publish on race in the 1790s, it is possible that a shift in his views on rightful labour relations – namely, the development of the right to a person akin to the right to a thing – generated his final rejection of slavery in *The Doctrine of Right* and *Perpetual Peace*, rather than a change in his views on race. With this framework in hand, Kant is finally able to articulate the distinctions between marriage and sex work, and between domestic servitude and slavery, which allows him to clearly ground, for the first time, an argument against slavery as inconsistent with Right. I take up Kant's arguments against slavery in Section 6.

As the argument in this section show, development of the 'right to a person akin to the right to a thing' framework allows Kant to map rightful relations of entitlement to sex and labour as well as their limits, distinguishing sex work and slavery as impermissible forms of use. In this formulation, access to sex, caregiving, and other domestic labour is a 'necessary' condition (Fey 27: 1381) to which independent men must be entitled, and so there must be a rightful form of this labour. As I will show in the next section, embedded in this framework is a rightful account of the relations of subordination with which Kant struggles in his anthropology and writings on race, which places women and non-whites in dependency relations through arguments for entitlement to their labour.

5 Labour, Leisure, and Laziness: A Kantian Taxonomy of Entitlement

'The human being is the only animal which must work', asserts Kant in the *Lectures on Pedagogy* (1803), arguing:

> He must first undertake many preparations before he can enjoy something for his living. The question whether heaven would not have cared for us more kindly if it had let us find everything already prepared so that we should not need to work at all, is certainly to be answered in the negative. For the human being requires occupations, including those that involve a certain constraint (Päd 9: 471).

Kant's insistence on the value of work as a particularly human activity, and his repeated claim that 'the best rest for him is that which comes after work' (Päd 9: 471), name the ways that labour is integral to the human condition, a universally valued dimension of human activity. But as we have seen, Kant's analysis of labour embeds a hierarchy both of labour and of entitlement to labour in his account of the rightful state. In this section, I tease out Kant's taxonomy of labour in order to show that his account of labour is consistent and continuous with his anthropological, geographical, and historical accounts of race and gender, providing a systemic and institutional justification for the dependency of women and non-whites.

Let us begin with Kant's thoughts on rest. The domestic sphere is valuable, he consistently notes in his anthropology lectures, because 'it is the only place where he can rest' (Anth-Frie 25: 702); while women are 'active and energetic' in their management of domestic matters, 'the reason why man loves domestic peace probably comes from the fact that he maintains the house as his place of rest' (Anth-Mensch 25: 1190). Men acquire servants, he notes in an early account of the household, 'from leisureliness' (while marriage arises 'from instinct' and parental right 'from duty' (J 19: 541)). This leisure is a *deserved* rest, which Kant describes as 'the highest physical good': 'the greatest sensuous enjoyment, which is not accompanied by any admixture of loathing at all, is resting after work' (Anth 7: 276). This sort of rest is designated as a feature of the domestic sphere, but it is specifically male. Kant notes that women, too, may outsource domestic responsibilities if their husbands are wealthy enough – to domestic servants (RDL 20: 465) and even to surrogates, as in Kant's reference to Parisian women who outsource their children's upbringing (Anth-Frie 25: 585); Kant would later refer to Parisian women as paradigmatic of civilized women (Anth-Mron 25: 1393).[28] But the household is the proper site for women's labour, just as the public and market spheres are for men's (Anth-Frie 25: 703); while men 'govern' in the household, determining the ends that dictate necessary labour, women 'put everything to work', executing and managing the labour to fulfil these ends (Anth-Frie 25: 702, 717). Thus, the labour of the household is not just in service of the householder's independence, but of his entitlement to rest and leisure, as well.

The definition of leisure as the 'highest physical good' that we find in the *Anthropology* is a refinement of Kant's earlier reflections on laziness. In earlier lectures, Kant describes laziness as a universal human propensity (Anth-Frie 25: 580), arguing that 'all labours are driven by the prospect of laziness, which puts them into motion' (Anth-Mron 25: 1420). But in the final textbook, Kant carefully distinguishes leisure from laziness, arguing that the former is 'a somewhat long refusal to go back to one's business and the sweet doing nothing for the purpose of collecting one's powers is not yet laziness: for (even in play), one can be occupied agreeably and usefully at the same time' (Anth 7: 276). Laziness, on the other hand, is 'the propensity to rest without having worked first' (Anth 7: 276).

---

[28] Kant adds that these Parisian women 'would gladly be relieved of bearing a child, and let another woman bear the child for her for money' (Anth-Frie 25: 585) are an example of the way in which natural drives are suppressed in conditions of civilization, and replaced by reason.

As Huaping Lu-Adler (2022b) has convincingly shown, laziness is a racialized trait in Kant's anthropological writings, from his early description of Blacks as 'lazy, soft, and trifling' (VRM 2: 438) to his later account of Blacks as 'disinclined to work', as evidenced by his infamous use of a pro-slavery tract in which the author claimed, in Kant's words,

> among the many thousand freed Negroes which one encounters in America and England he knew no example of someone engaged in a business which one could properly call *labour*; rather that, when they are set free, they soon abandon an easy craft which previously as slaves they had been forced to carry out, and instead become hawkers, wretched innkeepers, lackeys, and people who go fishing and hunting, in a word, tramps (GTP 8: 174 n).

Kant likewise references the laziness and 'weakness' of Native Americans, who 'are too weak for field labour' (VRM 2: 438 n) and are 'too weak for hard labour; too indifferent for industry' (GTP 8: 176). Laziness, Kant argues in the *Anthropology*, is 'the most contemptible' of the vices (Anth 7: 276).

Leisure, then, is the rest one is entitled to after hard work and laziness is the refusal to work, which functions as a justification for enslavement. But the argument is circular: if enslavement is justified by the apparent laziness of Blacks and Native Americans, the labour performed by the enslaved is never a justification for leisure. This valuation of labour is explicitly racialized, in that it is not confined to the enslaved, but to 'freed Negroes' as well: the Black freedman's labour is 'not what one could properly call labour' (GTP 8: 174 n) and his rest is always laziness.

Kant's distinction between leisure and laziness requires us to examine what activities register as labour on his account. We can note, first, that many of the activities women undertake within the household are considered *art*, rather than labour, from his early treatment of household duties in *Observations on the Beautiful and Sublime* (GSE 2: 236), to his discussion of the fine art of designing a dinner party in *Critique of Judgment* (KU 5: 306). We get a rare admission that women might do domestic labour in the *Anthropology*, where Kant admits that 'the feminine sex must train and discipline itself in practical matters; the masculine sex understands nothing of this' (Anth 7: 308); in earlier lectures, he specified that these practical matters are primarily 'the kitchen, childcare, and the sickroom' (Anth-Frie 25: 706).[29] For the most part, however, domestic labour is assumed to be the purview of servants.

---

[29] In early notes, (J 19: 470 *Refl* 7617), Kant refers to the 'work' ('*opera*') of childrearing, replacing the word 'choice'; his reference to childrearing as 'work' is clearly intentional. My thanks to Frederick Rauscher for this reference.

This analysis, developed as the bourgeois household emerged from the capitalist transformation of the feudal household, locates Kant's arguments in middle-to-upper class households, identifying the outsourcing of domestic labour as a key provision of access to independence. While this outsourcing was primarily gendered in lower class households as men increasingly worked outside the home, patterns of outsourcing in middle- and upper-class households enforced class differences, generating a class 'in service' to those qualified for political independence. And globally, this outsourcing was raced as the raw accumulation and production that generated European wealth and supported the rise of the bourgeois household was organized through colonialism and enslavement. The outsourcing of domestic labour is then a mark not only of wealth but of civilization: Kant notes that 'among unrefined groups of people the woman is a beast of burden' (Anth 7: 304 n), adding that 'in the crude state of nature . . . woman is a domestic animal. The man leads the way with weapons in his hands and the woman follows him loaded down with his household belongings' (Anth 7: 304). Notably, given the parallels established in the previous section between marriage and slavery, Kant's reference to the 'savage women' as 'a domestic animal' echoes an earlier note about slave labour, where he describes a slave as 'a domestic animal that is determined solely through the will of the owner' (J 19: 556 *Refl* 7925). It is through the outsourcing of domestic labour to servants or slaves (or, in contemporary times, to the service sector) that women can avoid being merely 'beasts of burden'.

Here, we see Kant's classed, raced, and gendered assumptions about labour constituting one another, ensuring that the femininity he identifies as 'proper' to women is accessed through outsourcing labour, and as such, is both raced and classed. Lower class women and 'savage women' are identified as 'beasts of burden', designed for the outsourcing of labour, both within their own communities and in the context of coloniality and enslavement. These comments reveal the degree to which it is not only class, but gender and race themselves, that are organized through labour. In the *Friedlander* lectures, Kant argues that 'if one takes unrefined nations, then the woman is not at all to be distinguished from the man; she does not have the charms which she has in the developed state, she must work by strength in just the same way as the man' (Anth-Frie 25: 699). For this reason, Kant insists, we can only study humanity, rather than the female sex, in the 'unrefined' state, since there is 'no difference in the character of the man and the woman in this state' (Anth-Frie 25: 699).

Therefore, the development of proper (white) womanhood is what 'makes the state refined' (Anth-Frie 25: 700; Anth-Mensch 25: 1189), and it is for this reason, Kant argues, that 'in anthropology the characteristic features of the female sex, more than those of the male sex, are a topic of study for the philosopher' (Anth 7: 303): proper womanhood is the mark of civilization. But Kant notes that it is not that civilization *produces* this femininity, rather, it is the condition in it can develop, while 'in the crude state of nature one can no more recognize these peculiarities than those of crab apples and wild pears' (Anth 7: 303). Kant's description of womanhood as 'developing' under favourable conditions echoes his account of the development of racial characteristics, marking proper womanhood as one of the core achievements of whiteness; his comparison of human sexual (in)difference in the state of nature to those of apples and pears emphasizes his insistence that women are barely distinguishable from men in a state of nature, and identifies 'savage' races as continuous with nature, much as, as Tiffany Lethabo King has argued, popular travel narratives of the seventeenth and eighteenth centuris often cast enslaved people as not only 'ungendered' but as features of the landscape, so that 'before the link between Black bodies . . . as labour could be naturalized, they had to momentarily function as vegetation' (King 2016: 1027). Through these arguments, in which Black women are *ungendered* as labourers (since they must labour 'with strength' as men do (Anth-Frie 25: 699)), even as they are *en-gendered* as reproductive beings (though their capacity for proper reproduction must be *managed*, just as crab apples and wild pears 'reveal their diversity only through grafting and inoculation' (Anth 7: 303)) we see Kant rehearse the arguments through which normative gender is revealed as a feature of whiteness (King 2016: 1028); gender, for Kant, is always raced.

Thus, of the two ends Kant claims nature has 'in establishing womankind', Black and 'savage' women fulfil only the former: 'the preservation of the species' (Anth 7: 305). The second end, 'the cultivation of society and its refinement by womankind', is specific to white women (Anth 7: 305). Proper womanhood is an achievement of whiteness, generated through the proper gendered organization of labour: the domestic sphere, as critical feature of civilization, is the 'favourable condition' under which the refinement of women's proper nature can occur. But the proper structure of this domestic sphere is equally critical: Kant notes that 'where women are excluded from society, as in the Orient, there the society of men is unrefined' (Anth-Frie 25: 706); this exclusion is later specified not merely as exclusion of women from the public sphere, but the lack of equal authority within the home (Anth-Frie 25: 717). This seclusion of women even within the home, then, is taken as a sign of a lack of civilization in Asian cultures, particularly in light of his claim that holding women in contempt is a sign of a lack of refinement (Anth-Mensch 25: 1189).[30]

---

[30] By way of contrast, Kant insists that among the Germans, 'women have always had a great influence on men, even those who still live in the forests. From this we can infer that they must

Kant's arguments on these points are remarkably consistent from his early notes to his final published text, though echoes of his practical philosophy shape his preoccupations. The 1775–6 Friedlander lectures, delivered as he developed his theory of race, emphasize distinctions between 'civilized', 'savage', and 'oriental' women, identifying the properly constructed domestic sphere as necessary to womanhood, which is marked as a feature of civilization and an achievement of whiteness. In the 1780s, as he was developing his popular essays on intellectual and political maturity, the Menschkunde (1881–2) and Mrongrovius (1884–6) lectures consider the public immaturity of women, noting that they can achieve domestic maturity only given a properly constructed domestic sphere; because of this lack, non-Europeans fail to achieve mature womanhood (Anth-Mron 25: 1299). Kant's final reflections, in the published *Anthropology from a Practical Point of View* (1798), hew most closely to his remarks in the early Friedlander lectures, suggesting that, as Stella Sanford has argued, Kant's views on gender were uncritically static in comparison to his views on race, perhaps because Kant did not understand these views, unlike his views on race, to be politically and scientifically charged (Sanford Forthcoming). But if Kant did not noticeably rethink his anthropological assessment of gender, he came to think systematically about its implications, embedding it within his practical philosophy: Kant's racialized understanding of gender is *made* political through the central role of domestic right and its attendant labour patterns in the trichotomy of Right.

Kant is likewise consistent in linking labour to civilization throughout his anthropological, historical, and geographical works. In the *Idea for a Universal History*, he defines civilization as an intergenerational labour (IaG 8: 20), while in the *Conjectural Beginning of Human History*, he argues that 'the human being was to labour himself out of the crudity of his natural dispositions' (MAM 8: 118) as he developed into the period of 'labour and discord' (MAM 8: 118), from hunter-gathering societies, to pastoral/agricultural ones, to the development of towns and their associated craftsmanship (MAM 8: 118–20).[31] If labour is a project of civilization, then the state of nature is coded as a state of laziness, in the 'shadowy image of a golden age ... the pure enjoyment of a carefree life, dreamt away in laziness or frittered away in childish play' (MAM 8: 122). 'One can still find such a life in Tahiti', Kant notes in the Mrongrovius lectures in a fit of Rousseaeuian romanticism, 'where laziness dominates all the inhabitants' (Anth-Mron 25: 1422). Civilization is thus possible only when 'the laziness was

---

not have been nearly so crude and uncivilized as the savages at present are in American and elsewhere ... .' (Anth-Mensch 25: 1190).

[31] Reinar Maliks (2014) has emphasized that Kant's argument here bears striking similarity to Adam Smith's conjectures regarding the development of human labour practices.

fought against and the human being was required to be industrious and hard working' (Anth-Mron 25: 1423). In the *Lectures on Pedagogy*, he emphasizes that the discipline of work is critical to the education of children, arguing 'it is of the greatest importance that children learn to work' (Päd 9: 470) although he adds, in a public essay written on the textbook used in his course, that this form of education is characteristic of the 'civilized countries of Europe' (ERP 2: 449).

Kant is consistent in deploying *laziness* to the freed slaves refusing to perform 'proper labour', the Native Americans performing domestic rather than field labour, and the colonized or enslaved Africans 'disinclined to work'; his references to *leisure*, while less systematic, repeatedly apply to the householder entitled to outsource domestic labour to wives, servants (and/or slaves). Taken together, these remarks reveal a persistent pattern of racing and gendering labour, mapping white European householders as always already entitled to the leisure of a job well done, and non-Europeans as always already lazy, as *never* entitled to rest. As is the case with Kant's assessment of gender, these are not merely anthropological observations, but are embedded in his theory of the state through his account of the independent citizen. Because labour is both a property of and a proof of civilization, the white European householder is always already entitled to rest, because he has always already done the labour of civilization; a primary function of education, as Kant suggests in his lectures on pedagogy, is to reproduce this entitlement in subsequent generations of white European men.

For Kant, then, labour is not primarily a mode of production, but a reproduction and legitimization of a particular political order. Labour's relevance lies in its ability to determine one's place in the relations of political society, framing independence and dependence as criteria for citizenship. And while labour is not a direct mode of accumulating land – Kant reminds us that mixing our labour with land is insufficient to make it ours (MM 6: 268) – it remains relevant to practices of accumulation: property ownership is the result of one's standing in a rightful state, and the organization of labour is a mechanism of establishing one's standing in the rightful state. Thus, it is not one's labour *on the land* that makes it yours but one's standing in the state. One's standing in the state is then *reproduced* through one's labour, which is the labour that entitles one to the great pleasures of rest and leisure in the wake of a job well done. And this entitlement to leisure is, of course, entitlement to the labour of others: of domestic servants, to wash one's clothes and cook one's food, of farm hands or sharecroppers or day laborers, who tend one's fields and produce one's food, of wives, who tend to one's sexual and emotional needs as well as to one's children. For Kant, this labour legitimizes the social and political order by reproducing the independence of the citizen; what is produced by this labour – the agricultural products, the homespun lace, the children and the citizen himself – register as the labour of the citizen, labour that further entitles him to rest, to leisure, to scholarship, reflection, and the time to make use of his reason.

These arguments reveal the ways in which, despite Kant's distinction between price and dignity and his claim that the value of human beings is not relative to 'universal human inclinations and needs' but is an absolute value (G 4: 434), he does identify differences in the value of labour, and in doing so, comes dangerously close to attributing market value to the human beings who do that labour. In his lectures on ethics, Kant makes explicit this valuation of labour, arguing, 'the distinctions of status elsewhere are those of external worth. The other avocations busy themselves with physical things, having only refer-ence to human life. The scholar, however, has a role whose main concern is to extend knowledge, and this seems to represent a different inner worth' (Eth-Col 27: 461). Though Kant extolls here the value of intellectual labour, he troubles the exceptionalism of scholarship a few lines later, where he adds 'scholars are thus the means to that end, and contribute something of value, but do not themselves have any superior worth thereby. Why should not a citizen, who is diligent and industrious in his calling, and otherwise does a good trade and keeps his house in order, have just as much worth as a scholar?' (Eth-Col 27: 462). The value of the scholar can be compared to that of the citizen – the *active* citizen, judging by Kant's reference to 'his good trade' and 'his house'. The value of the citizen and the scholar, expressed by a willingness to engage forthrightly in public reason (rather than treating 'the products of his under-standing as a merchant does his wares' (Eth-Col 27: 462)) operates as the standard to which others might 'work their way up' (MM 6: 315) even as it is a standard attainable only given a systemic reliance on, and entitlement to, reproductive and appropriated labour.

Kant's flirtation with attributing value not only to labour, but to the human beings who perform it, is particularly slippery given that he was writing at a time when human beings *did* have market value assigned to them through the global, institutionalized slave trade that shaped the emergence of capitalism and its labour system. Kant's own racialized reflections on labour and laziness reveal how deeply his account of labour was informed by the background conditions of the slave trade and global colonialism, while his carefully crafted theory of race included justifications of enslavement, and references to pamphlets defending slavery (GTP 8: 174 n).

As scholars have noted, however, Kant's political writings in the 1790s reveal a change of mind about slavery, from his reference to the 'cruelty' of the slavery in the sugar islands in 1795's *Toward Perpetual Peace* to his outright rejection of slave contracts as 'impossible' in 1797's *Doctrine of Right* (Kleingeld 2014; Valdez 2020; Lu-Adler 2022a). As I argued in the previous section, Kant's final development of rightful enclosed dependent labour in the form of domestic right may have armed him with a framework for definitively distinguishing between servitude and slavery, and thus, for rejecting slavery as inconsistent with innate right. But the structure of this argument was likely shaped by Kant's awareness of colonial conflict: Pauline Kleingeld has suggested that Kant's rejection of slavery may reflect his awareness of the developing revolution in Santo Domingue (Kleingeld 2014);[32] Ines Valdez has mapped the impact of colonial conflict, including the slave rebellion in Santo Domingue, on Kant's political philosophy (2020). Kant's careful conceptualization of rights to property as political, rather than as the outcome of labour, may also have been influenced by debates in Saint Domingue, as former slaves made their claim for political standing and their right to inherit the colony through their labour on its land. This appeal was expressly framed through reference to the Abbe Sieyès' distinction between active and passive citizenship, as emancipated slaves and leaders of the rebellion claimed that Black labour, both on plantations and the plots of land slaves farmed for subsistence, served as a justification for both rights to property and active citizenship (Dubois 2012, 33; Jackson 2014; Ravano 2020). If Kant was aware of these debates as part of the discourse about Sieyès' conception of citizenship, then his insistence that political standing produces the right to property – rather than the other way around – disrupts such claims to equal citizenship on behalf of the formerly enslaved. And, just as the abolition of slavery in Saint Domingue merely produced new forms of plantation labour (Dubois 2012; Ravano 2020: 730–2), Kant's rejection of slavery distinguishes rightful servitude from wrongful slavery without eradicating patterned reproductive and dependent labour: instead, Kant's arguments embed this labour and its attendant hierarchies in his account of the rightful state. In the next section, I explore how Kant circumscribes his rejection of slavery by carefully contrasting it to domestic labour. This circumscription, I argue, plays a critical role in delineating the limits of Kant's account of labour.

6 Kantian Reconstruction: Slavery, Abolition, and Poverty Relief

I turn now to Kant's arguments against slavery: his claim, in the *Doctrine of Right*, that slavery is 'impossible', since the slave 'will in fact have given

---

[32] Robert Bernasconi (2002), on the other hand, suggests that Kant recognized that his views on race were controversial, and kept them distinct from his moral and political philosophy for this reason, while Mark Larrimore argues that Kant didn't publish on race in the 1790s because his previous writings on race were by now well-established and frequently republished (2008: 358).

himself away, as property, to his master' (MM 6: 330). No person can be obligated by a slavery contract, since 'no one can bind himself to this kind of dependence, by which he ceases to be a person, by a contract, since it is only as a person that he can make a contract' (MM 6: 330). The slave contract is impossible in the same sense that the sex work contract 'is a contract that could not hold in right' (MM 6: 279). The problem, in both cases, is with the *form* of the contract: it matters not if the sex worker will be well-compensated nor whether the master treats the slave 'well'; in both cases, the contract itself is impermissible, and therefore cannot conclusively bind. This is because the sex worker and the slave enter a contract to give themselves up as things, to be 'used' as things (and not, importantly, to be used as *a mere means)* and thus cease to be the sorts of beings who can be bound by contract.[33] When I treat someone as a means only, I exploit them for my own ends; contracts are designed to *align* our relevant ends, ensuring that the relationship, or labour, in question is not exploitative. Using someone *as a thing* is not a form of exploitation, but of objectification; when it is also a failure to treat the person *as a person*, to recognize their right to humanity in their own person, then it is a problem of *fungibility*. Thus, Kant's objection to sex work and slavery is not that they are forms of exploitative labour, but that they are not labour at all: they are *use*. That slavery and sex work are so often used to reveal one another in Kant's arguments points to the ways that sexual use is a *feature* of slavery, embedded in the structure of slavery as *use*, rather than labour.[34]

---

[33] Feminists continue to debate whether it is productive to frame sex work as a form of labour: for a discussion of a range of issues surrounding sex work and body work as labour, see the essays collected in Wolkowitz et al. (2013). For an excellent example of Kantian scholarship on sex work as work, see Varden (2020), pp. 269–73.

[34] Kant defines slavery as an 'impossible' relation, 'the relation in terms of rights of human beings toward beings that have only duties and no rights' (MM 6: 241), claiming that 'these would be human beings without personality (serfs, slaves)'. The sex worker, by contrast, is described as 'surrendering herself as a thing to the other's choice' but retaining the right to 'cancel the contract as soon as [she] pleases' (MM 6: 279). Sex workers, then, retain their right to cancel the contracts that make them fungible in ways that slaves do not, so that sex work is not reducible to slavery. But because the slave has no such right to cancel contracts – this is, in fact, the core distinction between slavery and servitude (MM 6: 330) – the slave has no right to object to being subjected to sexual use: the slave has only duties to allow herself to be used, but no rights to determine the form of use (MM 6: 241). Sexual use, then, is a feature of slavery – and one that Kant was likely aware of, given the central role that hybridity plays in his account of racial formation: Kant's monogenetic theory of the races hinges on the claim in his 1775 essay on the human races that 'Negroes and Whites, while not different kinds of human beings (since they belong presumably to one phylum), are still two *different races* because each of the two perpetuates itself in all regions and both necessarily beget half-breed children or *blends* (mulattoes) with one another' (VRM 2: 430). Ten years later, Kant expanded his account of race mixing in order to argue that racial difference was unfailingly hereditary, but in doing so, he revealed a persistent awareness of the ways that white men had made sexual use of non-white women across the globe, arguing 'the white man with the Negro woman and vice versa produce the *mulatto*, with the Indian woman the *yellow* mestizo; the American with the Negro produce the

In this section, I show how sex work and slavery reveal the edges of Kant's theory of labour. Both sex work and slavery are remedied through the 'right to a person akin to the right to a thing', which is explicitly designed to resolve relations in which persons make use of one another as things by ensuring that in their rightful form, persons are used *as if* they are things. Just as the problem of sex work serves to justify Kant's account of marriage, the problem of slavery serves to justify his account of domestic labour. By framing the alternative to slavery as enclosed dependency, I'll argue, Kant's rejection of slavery resembles the arguments for slavery's abolition rehearsed in the passing of the Thirteenth Amendment. By taking a historical detour through political debates of American Reconstruction, I map the implications of Kant's argument against slavery for his broader accounts of labour, poverty, and political participation. This historical context allows me to identify the ways in which Kant's analysis of rightful labour rehearses arguments for ongoing relations of dependency that produce raced and gendered exclusion from public poverty relief programmes, as well as from public reason.

Understanding Kant's argument against slavery requires us to attend to the ways that it is discontinuous with Lockean and Marxist critiques that take slavery to pose a problem of exploitation. For Kant, the problem is that the enslaved person is treated as a thing, and so *ceases to be a person* (Fey 27: 1381; J 19 : 556; MM 6: 330), becoming instead 'a domestic animal that is determined solely by the will of the owner' (J 19: 556). This is then a problem that no regulation of labour can solve: the problem is not the *kind* or *amount* of labour the slave must perform, nor the conditions under which he must labour. Kant thus rejects the Lockean framework in which the master must be entitled to the labour of the servant or slave (since for Locke, the transformative power of this labour is critical to the accumulation of property).[35] Kant has no need of such an

---

black Caribbean, and vice versa. (The mixing of the Indian with the Negro has not been attempted.) ... The white father impresses on [the child] the character of his class and the black mother that of hers. Thus an intermediary sort of bastard must arise each time' (BBM 8: 95). Kant's long interest in racial hybridity as a key element of his monogenetic theory of the human races led him to carefully track practices of racial mixing, including the pervasive sexual use of Black, Indigenous, and Indian women through colonialism and slavery; the products of these unions are explicitly 'bastards' and their existence is implicitly justified by the fact that, as Kant argues in his account of the black Portuguese in Africa, 'how is it even probable that the first Portuguese that came there brought just as many white women with them, that those all stayed alive long enough, or were replaced with other white women' in order to reproduce (BBM 8: 105). Thus, it is reasonable to assume that Kant understood the degree to which forced sexual use and reproduction were persistent features of both racialized slavery and colonialism.

[35] In *The Second Treatise of Government,* Locke includes the labour of servants as an example of establishing rights to property: 'Thus the grass my horse has bit; the turfs my servant has cut; and the ore I have digged in any place, where I have a right to them in common with others, become my property, without the assignation or consent of any body. The labour that was mine, removing them out of that common state they were in, hath fixed my property in them' (Locke 2015,

argument, since labour is not an essential element of his theory of accumulation: property ownership turns on the state's recognition and authorization of one's right to own property, rather than, as Locke had it, labour itself. Kant's understanding of property as a *political* institution thus disrupts the Lockean linkage of labour and accumulation under the rubric of property, as well as the Marxian analysis of slavery as a form of alienated and exploited labour.

In order to clarify the distinctions between Kant's arguments against slavery and those developed in a Lockean or Marxist key, I compare Kant's arguments against slavery to frameworks developed within the Black radical tradition, which disrupt these Lockean and Marxist labour frameworks by locating slavery 'beyond the regime of labour', as Shona Jackson has put it (2014). By conceptualizing enslavement as a problem of *fungibility* distinct from exploitative labour, Frank Wilderson argues that while 'the worker labors *on* the commodity, s/he is not the commodity, his/her labour power is. Tragic as alienation in labour power is, it does not resemble the "peculiar character of violence and the natal alienation of the slave"' (Wilderson 2010: 69). In Kantian terms, this distinction can be understood as the difference between *exploiting* someone *as a means only* and making *use* of them as a *fungible thing*. Within the Black radical tradition, this distinction is crucial to understanding the legacies of slavery as 'predicated on modalities of accumulation and fungibility, not exploitation and alienation' (Wilderson 2010: 80). Sylvia Wynter argues that understanding this distinction reveals production as merely one aspect of domination, and labour as merely one measure of value in ways that disrupt Lockean and Marxist linkages between conquest, land, and labour (1992). This allows us to encounter enslavement as a form of domination that goes beyond labour, exploitation, and alienation.

Kant's account of the 'impossibility' of slavery points to this 'beyond'. He argues that conceptualizing slavery as labour is 'only a deceptive appearance' which masks stark domination: this domination cannot be captured by the frame of exploitative *labour*, since it is expressly the use of the enslaved person's body *as a thing*. The enslaved body is used as a thing, subject to the master's will, so that, as Saidiya Hartman puts it in her trenchant analysis of enslavement, 'the fungibility of the commodity makes the captive body an abstract and empty vessel vulnerable to the projection of others feelings, ideas, desires, values'

Second Treatise Chapter 5, Section 28); in his description of the household, he suggests that rights to the labour of one's servant, and rights to the labour of one's slave, are interchangeable: 'Let us therefore consider a master of a family with all these subordinate relations of wife, children, servants, and slaves, united under the domestic rule of a family ... (and the family is as much a family, and his power as paterfamilias as great, whether there be any slaves in his family or no)' (Locke 2015, *Second Treatise* Chapter 7, Section 86).

(1997: 21). This use of the enslaved is a violation of the right to humanity in the person, a form of use in which the enslaved is not only objectified as a thing, but made a fungible vessel for the master's will. For Kant, such a violation of innate right cannot be remedied through the institutions of acquired right: slavery, like sex work, cannot be made rightful through contract, which would authorize the master 'to use the powers of his subject as he pleases, he can also exhaust them until his subject dies or is driven into despair (as with the Negroes on the sugar islands)' (MM 6: 330). The enslaved are treated as things not just in the sense that they are *used*, but that they are *used up*: treated, like the sex worker, as *consumable* things (MM 6: 350). And so, slavery also poses problems of fungibility in that it necessitates practices of *replacement* and *accumulation*.

Despite Kant's reversals on slavery, his conceptualization of it as a problem of fungibility and accumulation is remarkably consistent. In a particularly horrifying passage from his 1780s geography lectures, he fixates on the problem of 'replacing' 20,000 slaves a year as they die from overwork, describing the solution as a slave trade in which 'Negroes ... catch each other, and one has to seize them with force.'[36] As he moves towards a critique of slavery in the 1790s, he identifies slavery as a *wasteful* mode of accumulation, troubling because it leads to 'partly the burial of a number of human beings *en masse* in the sea, partly the emptying of all coasts or also of whole peoples, and partly slow starvation through obstruction of the circulation of food' (VTP 23: 174). Slavery is wrong not because it *exploits* people, but because it *wastes* them.

But this framework means that Kant's rejection of slavery is then also a justification of the permissibility of labour relations, a delineation of permissible labour contracts made possible by locating slavery outside the frame. Slavery is here a mode of domination to be *left behind* in a rightful juridical order (other than, as we will see, in the form of prison or convict labour (MM 6: 333)). This move *beyond* slavery is particularly important because Kant is writing at what Wynter identifies as the moment of global transition from the accumulation of circulation (i.e., the era of global conquest and the rise of the slave trade) to the era of the accumulation of production (i.e., the era of industrialization and commercial plantations) (Wynter 1992). This is to say that Kant is writing as labour-power begins to *replace* the fungible body of captive persons as a measure of value: in Wynter's analysis, the commodity of

---

[36] 1782 lectures on Physical Geography, cited and translated in Kleingeld 2019: 'the Mandinka are the very most desirable among all Negroes up to the Gambia river, because they are the most hardworking ones. These are the ones that one prefers to seek for slaves, because these can tolerate labour in the greatest heat that no human being [Mensch] can endure. Each year 20,000 of this Negro nation have to be bought to replace their decline in America, where they are used to work on the spice trees.'

the fungible, enslaved body is labour's precursor, rather than an *aspect* of labour power (Wynter 1992: 81). Kant's own analysis of the economics of slavery reflects an awareness of this transition: consider his critique of slavery in the Sugar Islands not on the grounds that it is 'cruel and refined' but because it produces 'no direct profit' (ZeF 8: 359). In the drafts for this argument, Kant explicitly identifies enslavement as a project of accumulation that produces labour problems *for Europeans*: as the labour of European sailors and traders becomes the measure of value, the 'trade in negroes' has a negative impact on Europe owing to the 'amount of sea power and the increased numbers of sailors used' for commerce, trade, and war (ZeF 23: 174).

Thus, locating slavery outside the frame of labour nevertheless serves to buttress that frame. Here we can return to the parallels between Kant's account of slavery and of sex work, and to the development of 'the right to a person akin to the right to a thing' as the solution to these impossible forms of use. Just as marriage is posed as the rightful alternative to sex work, it is *domestic* labour that is marked as slavery's other, rather than contract labour. Just as Kant concludes that there can be no rightful *contract* organizing sexual relations, no contract can solve the problem of fungibility that slavery poses. Instead, Kant repeatedly locates slavery within his discussions of domestic right, from his early difficulties distinguishing slavery from servitude (Fey 27: 1380) to his analysis of marriage as the exception that proves the impossibility of slavery (Fey 27: 1336, 1379; J 19: 458). In the *Doctrine of Right*, Kant distinguishes the (rightful) domestic servant contract from the (impossible) slavery contract by saying 'the contract cannot be concluded for life but at most for an unspecified time, within which one party may give the other party notice' (MM 6: 283). Ironically, while marriage solves the problem of sexual use by embedding it in a *permanent* relation, domestic servitude solves the problem of slavery by configuring a *temporary* variant: 'someone can therefore hire himself out only for work that is determined as to its kind and amount' without 'thereby making himself a serf, whereby he would forfeit his personality' (MM 6: 330). What both arrangements have in common is a 'highly personal' arrangement designed to solve the problem of fungibility: where the slave has 'only duties but no rights' (MM 6: 241) and thus ceases to be a person, the domestic servant's personhood is protected by 'the right to a person akin to the right to a thing', ensuring that they *share* in the ends of the household, rather than being obligated to them 'like a domestic animal'.[37] Through this relation, fungible use becomes

---

[37] Kant's critique of slavery in the *Rechtslehre* is consistent with the Prussian Legal Code of 1794's law against slavery, which sought to distinguish domestic labour from slavery and serfdom by defining the relation between master and servant as a contract limited to a specific period of time for specific kinds of compensation. This emphasis on the contractual nature of domestic labour,

rightful labour, though the same performance of services is required. As in the case of sex work, the solution to slavery is not to eradicate the right to make use of another, but to find a *rightful* way to make use of them.

If slavery is impossible, it nevertheless serves (like sex work) to justify and clarify alternate modes of dependency as legitimate forms of labour. If the captive cannot agree to be owned as a thing, he *can* agree to be owned as a thing but used as a person: in this case, his master can make use of his powers as long as this does not amount to 'using them up' (MM 6: 283). Kant's discussion of the impossibility of slavery in the *Doctrine of Right* is organized explicitly to justify other forms of dependency: namely, to distinguish the impermissible use of persons as things from the permissible – indeed, rightful – right to persons *akin* to the right to things in the domestic sphere, from the rightful contracts that organize day labour and tenancy, and from the forms of 'holding' that arise when one takes a convict on as a bondsman (MM 6: 329–30). In the drafts for the *Doctrine of Right*, Kant includes 'the acquisition of a servant without contract through arrest for his debts', insisting that 'that is not the bondsmanship of a slave which can only transpire due to an offence' (VMM 23: 240).

These examples highlight the degree to which Kant's final and decisive rejection of rightful slavery is a careful defence of enclosed dependent labour. In other words, it is a map of alternate strategies of dependency, strategies which seek to replace the fungible ownership frame of the era of accumulation with the labour frame of the era of production (Wynter 1992). The explicit purpose of Kant's rejection of slavery, then, is not merely the transformation of the enslaved into labourers, but a set of political strategies designed to ensure that this labour is organized through dependence in ways that will not generate the lazy freedmen of *Teleological Principles* (GTP 8: 174 n), nor, as we will see, the public support of the lazy he decries in his argument for poverty relief (MM 6: 326).

At the same time, Kant's rejection of slavery is not total: even as he identifies the impossibility of private slave contracts, he justifies carceral slavery, arguing that

> whoever steals makes the property of everyone else insecure and therefore deprives himself (by the principle of retribution) of security in any possible property. He has nothing and can acquire nothing; but he still wants to live,

echoed in Kant, was a key provision that shifted Prussian legal frameworks away from the late feudal model, replacing the language of the *household* in the law with that of the *family*, signalling an emerging legal distinction between those bound by blood and those bound by labour (Gray 2000: 164). For further analysis of how Kant's account of the household responded to debates generated by the Prussian Legal Code of 1794, see Pascoe 2018.

and this is now possible only if others provide for him. But since the state will
not provide for him free of charge, he must let it have his powers for any kind
of work it pleases (in convict or prison labour) and is reduced to the status of
a slave for a certain time, or permanently if the state sees fit (MM 6: 333).

Carceral slavery is to be distinguished from private slavery because the
penal slave is subject to the will of the state, not to the private, arbitrary will
of the master. Private slavery, organized within the household, violates
innate right since, as Saidiya Hartman has put it, 'as property, the dispos-
sessed body of the enslaved is the surrogate for the master's body since it
guarantees his disembodied universality and acts as the sign of his power
and dominion' (1997: 21). But for Kant, this is an argument only against
private dominion: since the public will *is* 'disembodied universality', he
distinguishes between 'impossible' private slavery and *permissible* public
carceral slavery. Kant, in other words, presages the distinction that would be
written into American law, abolishing slavery except as punishment for
a crime.

6.1 A Thirteenth Amendment Kant

In order to clarify the position I am ascribing to Kant – and its implications –
I now take a historical detour. In the remainder of this section, I examine Kant's
arguments against slavery, as well as his account of poverty relief and public
reason, against the history of American Reconstruction. I read Reconstruction
through Saidiya Hartman's analysis of the 'afterlife of slavery', which examines
the abolition of slavery as a point of transition between modes of servitude and
subjection (1997: 5). Hartman locates the continuities between slavery and
Emancipation as being 'underwritten by black women's domestic labor'
(2016: 170), highlighting the ways in which racialized servitude is extended
through institutionalized insistence on the stability of racialized domestic labor.
By situating Kant anachronistically in this history, I argue that his argument
against slavery is what we might think of as a Thirteenth Amendment argument,
one that sought to abolish (private) slavery without addressing the authorization
of structural dependency built into the slave state; in the next subsection, I trace
the implications of Kant's argument through the Fourteenth and Fifteenth
Amendments, tracing the ways in which domestic labour plays a critical role
in configuring racial subjection in the wake of slavery. This history allows me to
read race and gender consistently into Kant's arguments, as well as to engage
with contemporary scholarship that has reconsidered Kant as a tool for racial
justice (Allais 2016; Mills 2017), often by situating him in the context of
Reconstruction (Valdez 2020; Basevich 2020; Fisette 2021).

I begin with the political debates that shaped the abolition of slavery. Hartman's analysis traces how these debates routinely located slavery as a domestic, rather than a political problem: a congressional debate about the Thirteenth Amendment posed the question, 'what is slavery? It is not a relation between the slave and the State; it is not a public relation; it is a relation between two persons whereby the conduct of the one is placed under the will of another. It is purely and entirely a domestic relation' (quoted in Hartman 1997: 173–4). In this argument, slavery is configured as a form of enclosed dependency, which obscures the state's role in legitimizing and institutionalizing it; its abolition then requires no reordering of the political, no development of new rights or relations. For Kant, as we have seen, the problem of slavery is likewise located within the domestic sphere: while he rejects slave contracts as 'impossible', he notes that a person can 'hire himself out . . . as a subject living on his master's property' (MM 6: 330). This requires no radical rethinking of the political order or the labour practices that organize it. Kant's rejection of slavery, like the Thirteenth Amendment's abolishment of it, rejects the law of chattel but not of personal right or enclosed dependency, and as we have seen, it too embeds a crucial exception to abolition: public, carceral slavery.

The abolition of private slavery posed economic challenges, just as the justification of carceral slavery turned on the state's refusal to 'provide for [the prisoner] free of charge' (MM 6: 333). Abolishing slavery would, in effect, generate a multitude of new potential dependents for the state. But if slavery was not a public institution but merely a wrongful form of personal right – a frame that Kant shared – then its abolition produced no public duties. Thus, with emancipation came the necessity of new strategies of bondage and subjugation, of generating non-wage labour relations and compulsory labour schemes (Hartman 1997: 127). These new strategies were necessitated by longstanding anxieties about whether or not Blacks would work when they were not coerced – anxieties parroted by Kant in *Teleological Principles*, where he insists that freed slaves refused to engage in activities 'that could properly be called labour' (GTP 8: 174 n), as well as anxieties about how public dependency programmes would then be abused by the indolent formerly enslaved, which were presaged in Kant's worry about poverty relief programmes unfairly benefitting the 'lazy' (MM 6: 326). Thus, Congress rejected legislation designed to provide public support to freedmen during Reconstruction as Senator James McDougall argued, 'if the negro, being made free, cannot take care of himself, how long shall we be his guardian, and take more care of him than we do the poor boys of our own race and people?' (quoted in Hartman 1997: 176). Emancipation, then, would require new strategies for enforcing the *enclosed* rather than the *public* dependency of freedmen, like the emergence of the sharecropping system, the convict-leasing system, as well as ongoing practices that outsourced domestic labour along race lines.

We find a map of such strategies in Kant's own reflections on slavery, which belie the binary of emancipation. We have seen how, in his early writings, he struggled to distinguish servitude from slavery, as well as to distinguish slavery from other forms of bondsmanship, including slavery as a form of punishment. Once slavery itself is removed from this frame – revealed as a condition of subjection that makes the enslaved merely a fungible body, 'a domestic animal', not to mention an enterprise whose economic viability had been exhausted – its variations remain. If slavery is defined as a person giving up his person for indeterminate labours in perpetuity and thus, as Kant puts it, ceasing to be a person, then its variations which do not meet these conditions – giving up one's person for *determinate* labours, or for indeterminate labours in pre-determined intervals, or for a determinate payment of a debt or a punishment, to do whatever is necessary for the welfare of the household – remain, bounded now by the insistence that this use of the person must be consistent with his status as a person, that this must be use of him *as a person*, and not a use that disposes of him. If slavery is abolished from the category of labour, its variations – unwaged labour, indebted labour, indentured labour, penal labour configured as convict-lease labour, sharecropping labour, domestic labour – need not be, and as Kant develops his rightful frame for the right to a person akin to the right to a thing, he carves out a space between enslavement and wage labour, a category that protects the exclusivity of independence and civil equality while ensuring ongoing entitlement to the labour that reproduces this independence.

6.2 A Fourteenth and Fifteenth Amendment Kant

As the abolition of slavery justified new forms of enclosed dependent labour, Kant's theory of labour can help us track the implications of these emergent patterns of dependency, including how raced and gendered exclusions from political participation and public reason are normed and enforced, ensuring the resilience of white patriarchal conceptions of justice. We see this, for example, in the frustrating limits of historical fights for suffrage: granting freedmen and women the right to vote does not transform labour relations or entitlements to dependent labour, nor does it transform practiced conceptions that dependency is a condition 'proper' to both women and people of colour. In this section, I compare Kant's arguments to those that informed discourse surrounding the Fourteenth and Fifteenth Amendments in order to show that the problem of exclusion is not simply that Kant's passive citizenship framework normalizes a political sphere in which some citizens – be they women, immigrants, or felons – are barred from participation. Rather, by organizing this exclusion through labour practices, Kant's framework ensures that the very practices that protect a white supremacist and patriarchal public sphere also provide the (under- or un-waged) labour that reproduces white supremacy and patriarchy. Thus, just as civil equality's requirement that each must have 'the right to work his way up' to civil independence does not disrupt the patterns of dependent labour that make that independence possible, the abolition of legally enforceable bondage does not transform the authorization of material inequality as consistent with legal equality.

Throughout Reconstruction, such authorizations of inequality were couched in the language of equality, as the Fourteenth Amendment granted freedmen 'the same remedies as white people', as Senator Edgar Cowan put it (quoted in Hartman 1997: 178). But these 'same remedies' did not target the structure of labour in the postbellum period, any more than the right to 'work his way up' altered the structure of domestic labour. Senator Cowan's appeal to equality as sameness elides the degree to which, as Hartman puts it, the 'abstract equality of rights bearers was achieved, in large measure, through black bondage' (1997: 119) just as, for Kant, the independence of active citizens was achieved, in large measure, through the enclosure of dependent labour. Indeed, these projects were closely intertwined, as women abolitionists-cum-suffragists would learn: the Fourteenth Amendment, which granted these 'same remedies' regardless of race, also inscribed gender discrimination into the Constitution, limiting these rights to 'male inhabitants', while the Fifteenth Amendment would grant the right to vote to all men – but not women – regardless of race. The exclusion of women from the Fourteenth and Fifteenth Amendments ensured that the domestic sphere – and its labour of dependency – would remain operative as the state's rejection of claims to public dependency for the emancipated instead gave way to new strategies of reproducing enclosed dependency (Hartman 1997). The laws granting civil equality enshrined – over the enraged opposition of women activists of all races – rightful discrimination based on gender, since gender discrimination was essential to authorizing the domestic as a sphere of enclosed and enforced dependency.

The logic of this argument is made explicit in Kant's account of poverty relief, which is *consistent with* his dependency argument. Kant's provision for poverty relief presumed that the structure of domestic dependency would limit the scope of the state's responsibility to provide relief. Kant's examples of the programmes providing poverty relief reveal the degree to which poverty relief targeted only those *without* access to enclosed dependency relations: widows who have lost their husband's protection, foundlings or children abandoned either because they were orphans or illegitimate (MM 6: 326–7).[38] Kant's subsequent comment that these programmes might be funded by taxing wealthy unmarried people (MM 6: 327) further underscores his assumption that the married are *already* providing this support to their dependents, including domestic labourers. Kant is explicit about this dependency in the drafts for the *Doctrine of Right*, where he argues that the domestic servant's 'status is regarded as dependent upon another's status, hence, his existence (regarding sustenance and protection)'; this produces 'the necessity of obedience due to the need for sustenance or maintenance as such: the domestic maintenance of dependents' (VMM 23: 327). If state poverty relief programmes are limited by patterns of enclosed dependency, then the state is vested in the perpetuation of these dependency relations.

We find an example of these practices in the New Deal's exclusion of domestic and agricultural workers from social security and other forms of state aid. Domestic and agricultural workers were, and are, overwhelmingly non-white, and their exclusion from labour laws has ensured that these forms of labour remain categorized as forms of enclosed dependency, and thus as *personal*, rather than public. These exclusions reflect a direct inheritance from institutionalized slavery, which primarily organized domestic and agricultural work; as we've seen, this pattern of labour is reflected in Kant, for whom both domestic and agricultural labour are prime examples of 'the right to a person akin to the right to a thing'. Domestic and agricultural workers have routinely been denied access to benefits and to minimum wage law, resulting in labour that is largely 'unofficial' and off-the-books; the precarity of this labour ensures exclusion from both participation in the public sphere and entitlement to state aid. These exclusions, in practice, targeted Black and, later, immigrant and migrant workers, ensuring that the 'good' dependency of social security and other New Deal programmes accrued primarily to white workers, while Black, Indigenous, and non-white immigrant workers became marked by

---

[38] Helga Varden and Sarah Holtman have offered alternate readings of Kant's poverty relief programmes, arguing that the right to poverty relief must be unconditional, since poverty relief is necessary to ensure that the poor do not find themselves arbitrarily subject to the choice of another (Varden 2008) by 'providing for needs foundational for agency' (Holtman 2018); this poverty relief must therefore be organized by the state through taxes on the wealthy, rather than through charity. I agree with Varden and Holtman that the Kantian case for poverty relief is most rigorous when it provides an escape route for dominative dependency, and that in this sense, it could be consistent with intervention in cases of domestic domination or abuse (Varden 2006b), but I think we need to contend with the ways Kant himself limited his vision for these programmes, and offered examples that point to domestic dependency as consistent with poverty relief. In this sense, my analysis is closer to the reading offered by Nuria Sanchez Madrid, who notes that Kant 'does not regard social dependence as unfair, provided it exhibits a fair social relation' (2019: 87).

'bad' dependency programmes that organize public discourse about welfare, immigration, and voting rights to the present day. Agricultural and domestic work have become primary markets for global migrant and trafficked labour, reflecting the degree to which enclosed dependent labour is shielded from state scrutiny and, thus, immigration law.

As Kantians attend to the obstacles white racism offers in the development of justice (Basevich 2020; Fisette 2021), Kant's theory of labour provides a critical lens for mapping strategies of political exclusion. Enclosed dependent labour shapes not only exclusion from public welfare programmes, but from public reason as well, since those who engage in enclosed dependent labour cannot, as we have seen, reason *as if* they were independent. Thus, Kant's account of rightful enclosed dependent labour organizes patterned political exclusion so that public reason remains *white* reason, as well as *male* reason. And this, in turn, ensures that the patterned inequalities embedded in this framework cannot be adequately scrutinized by public reason.

Thus, as these patterned exclusions have produced systemic poverty and strains on impacted communities, public discourse has continued, in a Kantian key, to emphasize the necessary function of the domestic sphere as a remedy for reliance on public welfare. In her analysis of the discourse surrounding supposed decline of the Black family, Kimberlé Crenshaw shows how this 'decline' is attributed to racialized overreliance on public welfare programmes and irresponsible Black female sexuality, so that the proposed solution is the production of proper domestic dependency within Black families, generated through economic reforms aimed at getting Black men to work and thus reducing the number of women-headed households and Black dependency on welfare (1989: 163–6). Saidiya Hartman maps variants of these arguments and the state surveillance practices associated with them during Reconstruction, when the domestic sphere was likewise cast as the alternative to dependency on public welfare (1997: 157–60). These resilient discourses, like contemporary welfare-reform policies, explicitly aim to reduce Black dependency on public welfare by reproducing the enclosed dependency of the domestic sphere, organized through a variant of the 'work his way up' model of the Black male head of household. In these arguments, Black women's dependency on public welfare is treated as indefensible since enclosed dependency within male-headed households, either white or Black, is mapped as 'proper' to them; the structural remedies proposed are designed to *ensure* the dependency of Black women, not to provide them with a path to independence (Crenshaw 1989: 166). This poses the question, which I address in the next section, of whether Black women, and other women of colour, are included in Kant's 'anyone can work their way up' account of civil equality.

This section has mined Kant's arguments against slavery in order to show how his linkage of slavery and domestic labour sheds light on strategies of political and economic exclusion in the wake of slavery, both in Europe and the Americas. We have seen that if slavery is most closely related to enclosed domestic labour, then its abolition does not produce independence or political standing, but opportunities to enforce new forms of 'rightful' dependency, like domestic labour, sharecropping, carceral forced labour, and migrant labour. These patterned forms of 'rightful' dependency are then crucial not just for limiting access to public welfare, but also to voting and public reason in ways that may have broad implications for the state's progress towards justice.

7 The Problem of Kantian Intersectionality

We come now to the crux of Kant's labour argument: namely, his insistence that asymmetrical forms of dependence are just, so long as 'anyone must be able to work his way up' (MM 6: 315). In the 1790s, this was a liberatory claim, proof that one's standing was limited by neither birth nor class, naming labour as the mechanism for advancement (MM 6: 329). But Kant's theorization of labour was nevertheless informed, as we have seen, by his anthropological, geographical, and historical arguments, which assumed *white male* entitlement to this right to work one's way up, and elided the ways that his theories of race and gender justified and enforced permanent patterns of dependence.

ˋ In this section, I argue that patterns of outsourcing domestic labour force us to consider how intersecting forms of oppression organize this right to 'work one's way up'. Thus, I make the case for intersectional analyses of Kant, showing how contemporary Kantians must reject readings of his political philosophy that locate domination in individual relations, tracked along single-axis frameworks of oppression.

We have seen how, when we attend to the labour practices that undergird Kant's conception of independence and maturity, it is apparent that access to caregiving and reproductive labour is a necessary (though not sufficient) feature of independence; entitlement to this labour is justified by Kant's insistence that anyone can 'work his way up'. But embedded in this argument is a refusal to account for what Pauline Kleingeld has called the 'compounded dependence' of those whose dependence is justified in multiple ways. Kleingeld notes that Kant gives no account of the position of *women* servants within the household, and never addresses their right to enter into nor terminate domestic labour contracts, given their gendered dependency. Nor, she argues, 'does Kant thematize the compounded dependence of female servants in the household – let alone that of female servants of colour' (2019: 10).

This is particularly troubling given the ways that women of colour have been systemically relegated to enclosed dependent labour, and the ways that their race and gender compound not only the formal features of those relations, but the forms of prejudice that serve to justify it. As these forms of prejudice compound one another, they produce positions of untenable and permanent dependency that undermine the distinctions normatively built into Kant's labour argument. Thus, Angela Davis describes the way that domestic workers have persistently organized to redefine their work 'by rejecting the role of the surrogate housewife. The housewife's chores are unending and undefined. Household workers have demanded in the first place a clear delineation of the jobs they are expected to perform' (Davis 1983: 230). Davis complicates here the key distinction Kant draws between unlimited enslaved labour and the limits placed on domestic labour to ensure its rightfulness, revealing how this elides the ways that *wives* have no clear delineation or limit on the kind of work they might have to perform. Thus, when *female* domestic workers are treated as 'surrogate housewives', this amorphous conception of domestic duty is extended to them, ensuring that their duties are both unprotected and unlimited, undermining the very distinctions between service and slavery on which Kant's account of labour rests.

Thus, while Kant's analysis of domestic labour attends to a domain dominated, then and now, by poor women and women of colour, his analysis of domestic labour nevertheless relies on what Kimberlé Crenshaw has called single-axis thinking (1989), a framework that assumes most women are wives and most servants (as workers) are men; his account of the dependence of servants and dependence of women as wives provides no direct analysis of women servants, nor of how the intersections of race and gender structure labour patterns. Though Kant provides us with no *explicit* account of the place of women of colour within his theory of right, we find an implicit account of the intersecting roles of raced and gendered dependency in his arguments for the right to 'work his way up'. Kant's assurance that political inequality is consistent with civil equality is structured remarkably similarly to what Kimberlé Crenshaw has called a 'but-for' argument, which prioritizes those who are privileged *but-for* their race or gender. In the 1989 essay in which she coined the term 'intersectionality', Crenshaw offers a second metaphor which maps directly onto Kant's 'work his way up' argument:

> imagine a basement which contains all people who are disadvantaged on the basis of race, sex, class, sexual preference, age and/or physical ability. These people are stacked – feet standing on shoulders – with those on the bottom being disadvantaged by the full array of factors, up to the very top, where the heads of all those disadvantaged by a singular factor brush up against the ceiling.

Their ceiling is actually the floor above which only those who are *not* disadvantaged in any way reside. In efforts to correct some aspects of domination, those above the ceiling admit from the basement only those who can say that 'but for' the ceiling, they too would be in the upper room. A hatch is developed through which those placed immediately below can crawl. Yet this hatch is generally available only to those who – due to the singularity of their burden and their otherwise privileged position relative to those below – are in the position to crawl through. Those who are multiply-burdened are generally left below unless they can somehow pull themselves into the groups that are permitted to squeeze through the hatch (1989: 151–2).

Crenshaw's basement analogy points to the limits of the 'work his way up' argument, to the ways in which it applies only to those facing a single point of discrimination or, to put it differently, those standing on the shoulders of others. Thus, arguments focused on gender discrimination can insist that women, too, can 'work their way up' while arguments focused on race discrimination insist that the liberation of the Black community turns on the ability of Black *men* to 'work their way up'. But as my analysis of Kant's theory of labour has shown, claims that individual wives or servants can 'work their way up' does not produce an argument for eradicating domestic or dependent labour; instead, it shifts that labour down what Arlie Hochschild has called a care chain (2001). Care chains track the privatized outsourcing of domestic labour, giving a name to the ways that caregiving labour produces derivative vulnerabilities that are likewise passed down the care chain (Fineman 2005), which can be understood, in light of Crenshaw's basement analogy, as passing labour down the chain of people standing on one another's shoulders.

Crenshaw's basement analogy names the ways that Black women are impacted, as legal theorist Pauli Murray put it, 'by both Jim Crow and Jane Crow', so that Black women bear both the double disenfranchisement of their race and gender, as well as cultural stereotypes born at their intersection: 'the stereotypes of female "dominance" on the one hand and loose morals on the other, both growing out of the roles forced on them during the slavery experience and its aftermath' (Murray 1947). Kristie Dotson conceptualizes 'Jane Crow' as a position of simultaneous *structural* invisibility and hyper-visibility 'beneath warring systems of privilege e.g., white and male supremacy' (Dotson 2017: 420–1). Thus, 'in Jane Crow subordination, there are malfunctions with respect to "assumptions, stereotypes, custom, and arrangements" that work together to submerge and leave relatively defenceless entire populations' (Dotson 2017: 421). When we read Kant's account of domestic right in light of his anthropological and historical theories of race and sex, we can identify the ways that domestic right operates through such a set of 'assumptions, stereotypes, custom, and arrangements' that place women of colour in systemically untenable positions within enclosed dependency.

Reading Kant's theory of labour through the lens of 'Jane Crow' and intersectionality draws our attention to the ways that political oppression and economic exploitation co-constitute one another, challenging Kant's assertion that the 'right to a person akin to the right to a thing' is voluntary in ways that make it fully consistent with right. Rather, we might think of it as what Nancy Folbre has called the 'coerced cooperation' of reproductive labour (2020: 548). This captures the cooperative dimension that Kant's account emphasizes: the reciprocal obligations, the shared ends, the quasi-contractual basis of such relations. But it draws our attention to the ways in which, if dependent labour is a necessary feature of a political order, then economic, institutional, and social coercion will operate to ensure ongoing access to dependent labour. The problem is not that any given domestic labour arrangement is an instance of being bound by another in ways they could not bind us, but that coercive background conditions ensure that those who enter into these arrangements have few other options. This belies the binary between voluntary and dominative relations, revealing how intersections of multiple systemic oppressions enforce forms of dependency that maintain broader patterns of domination. This may look like the discriminatory hiring practices that kept Black men and women out of forms of labour with benefits, unions, and good wages and thus kept them tied to the dependency of domestic and agricultural labour; it may look like immigration policies that create a migrant underclass concentrated in domestic, agricultural, and other 'informal' labour markets; and it may look like culturally dominant 'controlling images', to use Patricia Hill Collins' term, that operate – within a US context – ensure that Black women 'know their place' in the care chain, granting respect and access to social capital to the 'mammy' archetype who works to support white families while vilifying Black mothers as welfare queens and Jezebels (Hill Collins 1989).[39]

When we analyze these systemically untenable positions through frameworks that cast dependency as a *personal*, rather than a *political*, project, we obscure the coercion that organizes supposedly cooperative (and thus, *rightful*) labour relations. We elide the coercion embedded in domestic labour by casting domestic relations as *personal*, *intimate*, and *special*. We have seen how Kant constructs marriage as necessary (and special) precisely because it remedies the

---

[39] While these examples examine the systemic forces that produce untenable forms of dependency in the United States, and focus on the positions and perspectives of Black women, similar systemic forces coerce the labour of other women of colour and ethnicized women in other social and political contexts. Frameworks like intersectionality and Jane Crow offer us tools to identify these coercive patterns across social and political contexts.

fungible nature of sexual objectification by organizing sex through the highly specific right to one person. The intimacy of the domestic sphere is likewise mapped as the particular, highly personal, right to one's spouse, to one's children, along with the corresponding duties to support and protect them. The specificity of these relations is what justifies the enclosure of the domestic realm, figuring it as a space in which non-fungible labour takes place, labour that could not therefore be made public or organized in common since it is *personal*: it is care, love, intimacy.

Except that, of course, Kant's own account of the right to outsource domestic labour reveals the fungibility within the domestic sphere: it does not matter who does domestic labour, so long as it gets done (and so long as it gets done in ways that do not disrupt the householder's claim to independence). This logic of domestic fungibility organized the feudal and slaveholding households, even as talk of 'highly personal rights' to one's servants and slaves obscured it; it is embedded in the bourgeois household and the modern nuclear family by arguments like Kant's that blur the specificity of sexual and parental right with the organization of domestic labour; it is inherited by liberal feminism, in its insistence that women can 'work their way up' by simply outsourcing caregiving and domestic labour. Thus, the lack of juridical protections institutionalized in this 'new star' in Kant's juristic heavens are reproduced in contemporary legal frameworks, where domestic workers and non-parental caregivers have few rights and legal recognitions (Murray 2008). These patterned exclusions produce persistent practices of orienting solidarity and support away from those who provide this labour, even within feminist contexts, obscuring the coerced cooperation that organizes practices of outsourcing (Pascoe 2015).

These patterns of coerced cooperation are fractal (brown 2017; Folbre 2021), repeating from individual households to global patterns of migrant labour, clarifying the ways that in Kant's time and our own, the 'independence' of Enlightenment and 'development' of contemporary globalization in fact rely upon entitlement to exploited and extracted labour across the globe. Attending to Kant's arguments about domestic labour can help us to identify these fractal patterns, elaborated from strategies practiced within the household which generate enclosed dependent labour through care chains, which produce 'care drains' as caregiving labour shortages emerge at the bottom of the care chain, producing raced and classed patterns of vulnerability and dependency, since the support of caregiving labour is then unavailable in the communities at the bottom of the care drain (Ehrenreich 2003).

We saw particularly clear examples of these patterns in the Covid19 pandemic, which strained care chains around the globe, disrupting the logic of fungibility that undergirds practices of outsourcing care. As schools, childcare, and eldercare facilities closed, women found themselves taking on disproportionate amounts of childcare and other domestic labour, even as those paid, in normal times, to provide this labour found themselves unemployed and struggling to make ends meet. At the same time, the pandemic revealed the degree to which disaster labour is predominantly caregiving labour, disrupting both gendered assumptions about the labour of disaster (Luft 2016; Pascoe and Stripling Forthcoming) and claims that pandemics are 'a great equalizer'. Instead, 70 per cent of the global healthcare workforce is female (Miyamoto 2020). In the United States, more than 50 per cent of the caregiving and service labour deemed 'essential' or 'key' in the pandemic was performed by women of colour, who have long been the majority of caregiving, service, and domestic workers, thanks to the politics of enclosed dependency; this patterning both exacerbated the inequitable impact of Covid19 within communities of colour, and revealed the deep precarity of workers in these fields (Obinna 2021; Rho et al 2020). Care chains, organized through coerced cooperation, operate as drains of resilience in ways that existent policy frameworks have systemically ignored: pandemic preparedness in the United States had failed to account for caregiving, as the United States Centers for Disease Control planned for school closures but not for the surges in caregiving associated with them (Pascoe and Stripling 2020). Meanwhile, the dominant predictive frameworks used to map the spread of Covid19 across regions in the United States excluded caregiving networks from their account of 'linking' social capital, meaning that primary vectors like schools, day cares, camps, and the flow of vulnerability down privatized care chains were unaccounted for (e.g. Fraser et al 2021; Pascoe and Stripling Forthcoming). The lack of attendance to caregiving in pandemic planning is a reflection of our practiced refusal to engage in systemic analyses of domestic labour, of the ways in which patterns of outsourcing care produce vectors of vulnerability and, in a pandemic, contagion (Pascoe and Stripling 2020).

Thus, the raced and gendered impacts of the pandemic reveal both the necessity of juridical and philosophical frameworks for attending *systemically* to domestic and caregiving labour, and the critical need for intersectional methodologies in theorizing the distribution of caregiving and its attendant patterns of vulnerability through patterns of coerced cooperation. When we understand Kant's theory of labour to include a careful theorization of the domestic, and to be informed by his theorization not only of race and gender, but of key structural linkages between them, then his analysis of labour may offer insights for addressing both these problems. In this way, I identify Kant's theory of labour as a useful site for generating what Nancy Folbre has called 'an intersectional political economy', which 'redefines "the economic" in ways that encompass both reproduction and social reproduction, including the creation of human capabilities and the social institutions that bind people into groups with at least some common ideas and interests' (Folbre 2021). Kant's theory of labour allows us to think beyond inherited Marxian frameworks, since Kant is not bound by Marxist distinctions between 'productive' and 'reproductive' labour (Pascoe 2017). Rather, Kant is writing at a moment before 'labour' is located outside the home, during an era when a considerable portion of economic production occurs within the household, be it the late feudal home, the home-work economy, or the colonial and plantation economies, where production was largely organized through patterned domestic labour (in the sense that slaves and serfs were located under *personal* right); even as industrialization and global trade expanded, primitive accumulation and the production of raw materials, at both small scales within communities and at the global level, remained organized through 'domestic' labour practices. For Kant, domestic labour was an integral element of the economy, one that required a distinctive place in the system of right.

Kant's theory of labour, then, does not merely trouble the ways that Kant's political theory relies on his social and anthropological theory. In tracing patterns of exclusion in the Kantian state, I am not asking whether his theory of race or gender could be excised or subject to the scrutiny of public reason, generating an anti-racist, feminist variant of the Kantian political state. Rather, I am pointing to the ways that his social theory is rendered normative by his conception of civil independence. Thus, I am asking how we would need to theorize Kantian independence differently in order to make it possible to work towards a more just conception of the state. I have argued that Kantian arguments that seek to be accountable to intersectional theorizing must reject readings of his political philosophy that locate domination in individual relations, and develop systemic analyses of the ways that structural and fractal domination is built into normative concepts like independence, public reason, and the political sphere itself, through patterns of coerced cooperation and outsourcing that perpetuate local and global patterns of intersectional inequality, including Jane Crow and the care drain. These patterns are fully visible only when we bring an intersectional lens to our analysis, refusing the 'basement logic' that provides an escape hatch, or a way to 'work one's way up' only to those standing on the shoulders of others.

Thus, we must learn to interrogate Kant's principles from the perspectives of those who are multiply disenfranchised by the systems in question, such as those who do the daily labour of reproducing citizens and, by extension, the state itself. From this perspective, civil independence is revealed as a condition of *interdependence*, with reproductive and caregiving labour recognized as central to the project of justice. This allows us to ask whether the insight we should draw from Kant's formulation of innate right as 'independence from being bound by others to more than one can in turn bind them' (MM 6: 237) is not the illusory ideal of civil and material independence as characteristic of the Kantian political agent, but rather the fact of our interdependence as beings who are bound to, and thus dependent upon, one another.

8 Concluding Remarks: Kantian Systemic Injustice

Kant's account of justice is famously systemic, developing an institutional account of the state designed to support freedom and prevent domination. But Kant's accounts of domination and oppression are pointedly *not* systemic, relying either on his anthropological arguments about gender and his theory of race, or on claims about individual immaturity (WIE 8: 35; GTP 8: 174 n). This gap informs contemporary claims that Kant's theory of justice can be reconstructed or rescued from concerns about raced or gendered oppression, since it does not *structurally* embed this oppression, relying on it only empirically, historically, or circumstantially. These claims rely on a species of Kant's own rejection of the idea that there are 'special duties that we have to particular kinds of people, namely, duties in regard to difference of age, sex, and station' since 'all these duties are deducible from the foregoing duties to mankind' (Eth-Col 27: 461). This move anticipates contemporary reconstructive arguments that seek to reclaim or radicalize Kant, sidestepping questions of gendered, raced, or colonial oppression.

Centring Kant's analysis of labour disrupts this move, mapping the structures of oppression *within* his theory of freedom and unmasking them by troubling civil equality's requirement that 'anyone can work his way up' as a remedy for the exclusionary conditions that structure civil independence. Kant's manservant Lampe's right to 'work his way up' does not transform Kant's entitlement to the labour of a servant to make possible the conditions of his independence. Each individual freedman's right to 'work his way up' does not transform the logics of a racialized state or colonial empire in which the material conditions of independence rely on a sizeable domestic/colonial staff dedicated to 'doing whatever is necessary for the good of the household'. Each individual woman's right to seek a profession and participate in public life does not transform our collective reliance on the labour of caregiving and social reproduction, which is then outsourced through informal domestic labour: to other women, to domestic labourers who are, globally, overwhelmingly women of colour and undocumented immigrants/noncitizens, to the semi-private sphere in which predominantly women of colour perform reproductive labour in day-cares, laundromats, personal grocery shopping, home-cleaning services, and so on. These cases reveal the structural domination lurking in Kant's account of civil equality, and the coerced cooperation that underwrites his conception of civil independence.

I have shown that attention to Kant's 'trichotomy' argument, which develops a nuanced account of the structure of labour and gender at a critical historical juncture, offers several resources and interventions to contemporary Kantian and feminist scholarship. Feminist thinking interested in adapting and reconstructing Kantian arguments can learn from Kant's own careful theorization of labour, which provides a reminder that attendance to labour practices can unmask the patterns of oppression embedded in liberal and neoliberal frameworks. Such feminist arguments may find Kant's insistence on a trichotomous structure of Right useful to challenging the contemporary feminist reliance on the public/private distinction, which tends to blur distinctions between the public and market spheres in ways that have been useful to the development of neoliberalism and late capitalism. Kantian scholarship can learn from Kant's own careful thinking about the tensions between marriage and slavery in order to trouble contemporary scholarship that takes up questions of race/racism and sex/gender separately, and instead develop long-overdue attendance to the ways that Kant's conception of the independent (and autonomous) subject is intersectionally constructed through *both* raced and gendered assumptions of entitlement and exclusion.

At the same time, thinking about Kant's raced and gendered exclusions as co-produced through his accounts of labour and independence ensures that we do not produce false categories of inclusion, such as assuming that women can 'work their way up' without attending to the racialized outsourcing of caregiving and reproductive labour at both the local and global levels, in Kant's time and our own. As we struggle to make Kantian philosophy accountable to intersectional and decolonial theorizing, Kant's theory of labour provides a starting point for locating intersectional inequalities in Kant's thinking, for disrupting the 'single-axis' thinking that continues to predominate in Kantian scholarship, and for identifying the structural forms of domination embedded in his practical philosophy.

In the wake of a global pandemic that strained caregiving networks across the globe while revealing this very labour as 'essential' to survival, Kantian arguments that insist on 'the foregoing duties to mankind' without analysis of how inequity, exclusion, and entitlement are patterned through labour, law, and institutional oppression are not drawing on the full resources of Kant's political philosophy. Thus, I think it is worth thinking about Kant on labour. Doing so forces us to engage the materiality of his political philosophy, rather than allowing the concrete conditions of freedom to be abstracted to an idealized account, reducing labour to a relation of rights. Kant's theory of labour provides us with a starting point for reconceptualizing *interdependence* as the full political expression of right to humanity in the person, and reconsidering, from an intersectional perspective, what material and institutional arrangements best support our freedom and equality *as human beings*.

References

Primary Sources: Works by Kant

Anth *Anthropology from a Pragmatic Point of View*. Edited and translated by Robert Louden. Cambridge University Press, 2006. AA7: 127–333.

Anth-Frie 'Anthropology Friedländer'. In *Lectures on Anthropology*, edited by Allen Wood and Robert Louden. Cambridge University Press, 2012, pp. 37–255. AA25: 469–728.

Anth-Mensch 'Menschenkunde'. In *Lectures on Anthropology*, edited by Allen Wood and Robert Louden. Cambridge University Press, 2012, pp. 281–333. AA25: 853–1203.

Anth-Mron 'Anthropology Mrongovius'. In *Lectures on Anthropology*, edited by Allen Wood and Robert Louden. Cambridge University Press, 2012, pp. 335–509. AA25: 1209–1429.

BBM 'Determination of the Concept of a Human Race'. In *Anthropology, History and Education*, edited by Günter Zöller and Robert Louden. Cambridge University Press, 2007, pp. 145–59. AA8: 89–106.

ERP 'Essays Regarding the Philanthropinum'. In *Anthropology, History and Education*, edited by Günter Zöller and Robert Louden. Cambridge University Press, 2007, pp. 98–103. AA2: 447–52.

Eth-Col 'Moral Philosophy: From the Lectures of Professor Kant, Taken by Georg Ludwig Collins'. In *Lectures on Ethics*, edited by Peter Heath and J. B. Schneewind. Cambridge University Press, 1997, pp. 37–221. AA27: 243–472.

Eth–Vigil 'Notes on the Lectures of Mr. Kant on the Metaphysics of Morals, Taken by Johann Friedrich Vigilantius'. In *Lectures on Ethics*, edited by Peter Heath and J. B. Schneewind. Cambridge University Press, 1997, pp. 250–452. AA27: 479–732.

Fey 'Natural Right Course Lecture Notes by Feyerabend'. In *Lectures and Drafts on Political Philosophy*, edited by Frederick Rauscher. Cambridge University Press, 2016, pp. 73–180. AA27: 1317–94.

GMS 'Groundwork of the Metaphysics of Morals'. Edited by Thomas Hill and Arnulf Zweig. Translated by Arnulf Zweig. Oxford University Press, 2002. AA4: 387–463.

GSE 'Observations on the Feeling of the Beautiful and Sublime'. In *Anthropology, History and Education*, edited by Günter Zöller and Robert Louden. Cambridge University Press, 2007, pp. 18–62. AA2: 205–55.

GTP 'On the Use of Teleological Principles in Philosophy'. In *Anthropology, History and Education*, edited by Günter Zöller and Robert Louden. Cambridge University Press, 2007, pp. 195–218. AA8: 158–83.

IaG 'Idea for a Universal History with a Cosmopolitan Aim'. In *Anthropology, History and Education*, edited by Günter Zöller and Robert Louden. Cambridge University Press, 2007, pp. 107–20. AA8: 15–31.

J 'Reflections on the Philosophy of Right'. In *Lectures and Drafts on Political Philosophy*, edited by Frederick Rauscher. Cambridge University Press, 2016, pp. 1–72, with additional unpublished translations provided by Fred Rauscher, using Akademie Pagination. AA 19: 325–613.

KU *Critique of the Power of Judgment*. Edited by Paul Guyer and Eric Matthews. Translated by Paul Guyer. Cambridge University Press, 2002. AA 5: 167–485.

MAM 'Conjectural Beginning of Human History'. In *Anthropology, History and Education*, edited by Günter Zöller and Robert Louden. Cambridge University Press, 2007, pp. 160–75. AA8: 107–23.

MM 'The Metaphysics of Morals'. Edited and translated by Mary Gregor. Cambridge University Press, 1996. AA6: 211–491.

Päd 'Lectures on Pedagogy'. In *Anthropology, History and Education*, edited by Günter Zöller and Robert Louden. Cambridge University Press, 2007, pp. 437–85. AA9: 437–98.

RDL 'Remarks on the Doctrine of Law'. In *Lectures and Drafts on Political Philosophy*, edited by Frederick Rauscher. Cambridge University Press, 2016, pp. 341–54. AA20: 446–66.

TP 'On the Common Saying: That May be Correct in Theory, But It Is No Use in Practice'. In *Toward Perpetual Peace and Other Writings on Politics, Peace, and History*, edited by Pauline Kleingeld. Yale University Press, 2006, pp. 44–66. AA8: 289–313.

VMM 'Drafts for the Metaphysics of Morals'. In *Lectures and Drafts on Political Philosophy*, edited by Frederick Rauscher. Cambridge University Press, 2016, pp. 233–358. AA 23: 246–359.

VRM 'Of the Different Races of Human Beings'. In *Anthropology, History and Education*, edited by Günter Zöller and Robert Louden. Cambridge University Press, 2007, pp. 82–97. AA2: 427–52.

VTP 'Drafts for Theory and Practice'. In *Lectures and Drafts on Political Philosophy*, edited by Frederick Rauscher. Cambridge University Press, 2016, pp. 191–206. AA 23: 127–43 and Stark 244–5.

VZF 'Drafts for Toward Perpetual Peace'. In *Lectures and Drafts on Political Philosophy*, edited by Frederick Rauscher. Cambridge University Press, 2016, pp. 207–26. AA 23: 155–92.

WIE 'What Is Enlightenment?' In *Toward Perpetual Peace and Other Writings on Politics, Peace, and History*, edited by Pauline Kleingeld. Yale University Press, 2006, pp. 17–23. AA 8: 35–42.

ZeF 'Toward Perpetual Peace'. In *Toward Perpetual Peace and Other Writings on Politics, Peace, and History*, edited by Pauline Kleingeld. Yale University Press, 2006, pp. 67–109. AA8: 341–86.

Secondary Sources

Achenwall, Gottfried. (2021). *Natural Law: A Translation of the Textbook for Kant's Lectures on Legal and Political Philosophy*. Edited by Pauline Kleingeld, translated by Corinna Vermeulen. Bloomsbury Press.

Allais, Lucy. (2016). Kant's racism. *Philosophical Papers*, *45*(1–2), 1–36.

  (2015). What properly belongs to me. *Journal of Moral Philosophy*, *12*(6), 754–71.

Altman, Matthew. (2010). Kant on sex and marriage. *Kant-Studien*, *101*, 309–30.

Basevich, Elvira. (2020). Reckoning with Kant on race. *The Philosophical Forum*, *51*(3), 221–45.

Beiner, Ronald. (2011). Paradoxes in Kant's Account of Citizenship. In Charlton Payne and Lucas Thorpe, eds, *Kant and the Concept of Community*. University of Rochester Press, pp. 209–25.

Bernasconi, Robert. (2011). Kant's Third Thoughts on Race. In Stuart Elden and Eduardo Mendieta, eds, *Reading Kant's Geography*. SUNY Press, pp. 291–318.

  (2002). Kant as an unfamiliar source of racism. *Philosophers on Race: Critical Essays*, 145–66.

Bohrer, A. J. (2019). *Marxism and Intersectionality*. Verlag.

Boxill, Bernard. (2017). Kantian Racism and Kantian Teleology. In Naomi Zack, ed., *The Oxford Handbook of Philosophy and Race*. Oxford University Press, pp. 44–54.

Bramer, Marilea. (2010). The importance of personal relationships in Kantian moral theory: a reply to care ethics. *Hypatia*, *25*(1), 121–39.

brown, adrienne maree. (2017). *Emergent Strategy*. AK Press.

Brown, Heather. (2012). *Marx on Gender and the Family*. Haymarket Books.

Byrd, B. S. (2002). Kant's Theory of Contract. In Mark Timmons, ed., *Kant's Metaphysics of Morals: Interpretive Essays*. Oxford University Press, pp. 111–32.

Cash, Mason. (2002). Distancing Kantian ethics and politics from Kant's views on women. *Minerva: An Internet Journal of Philosophy*, *6*, 1–21.

Copeland, Roy. (2010). The nomenclature of enslaved Africans as real property or chattels personal. *Journal of Black Studies*, *40*(5), 946–59.

Crenshaw, Kimberlé. (2011). From private violence to mass incarceration: thinking intersectionally about women, race, and social control. *UCLA Law Review*, *59*, 1418.

(1991). Race, gender, and sexual harassment. *Southern California Law Review*, *65*, 1467.

(1989). Demarginalizing the intersection of race and sex: a black feminist critique of antidiscrimination doctrine, feminist theory and antiracist politics. *University of Chicago Legal Forum*, Article 8, 139.

Davis, Angela. (1983). *Women, Race, and Class*. Random House.

Deligiorgi, Katerina. (2005). *Kant and the Culture of Enlightenment*. SUNY Press.

Denis, Lara. (2001). From friendship to marriage: Revising Kant. *Philosophy and Phenomenological Research*, 63(1), 1–28.

Dotson, Kristie. (2017). Theorizing Jane Crow, theorizing unknowability. *Social Epistemology*, *31*(5), 417–30.

Dubois, Laurent. (2012). *Haiti: The Aftershocks of History*. Metropolitan Books.

Ehrenreich, Barbara, and John Ehrenreich. (1979). The Professional-Managerial Class. In Pat Walker, ed., *Between Labour and Capital*. Southend Press, pp. 5–49.

Ehrenreich, Barbara, Arlie Hochschild, and Shara Kay. (2003). *Global Woman: Nannies, Maids, and Sex Workers in the New Economy*. Macmillan.

Engels, Friedrich. (2010). *The Origin of the Family, Private Property and the State*. Penguin Books.

Eze, Emmanuel Chukwudi. (1995). 'The Color of Reason: The Idea of "Race" in Kant's Anthropology'. *The Bucknell Review*, *38*(2), 200.

Federici, Sylvia. (2020). Re-enchanting the world. *Journal of International Women's Studies*, *21*(1), 409–12.

(2013). *Revolution at Point Zero: Housework, Reproduction, and Feminist Struggle*. PM Press.

(2004). *Caliban and the Witch*. Autonomedia.

Ferguson, Ann. (1979). Women as a New Revolutionary Class in the US. In Pat Walker, ed., *Between Labour and Capital*. Southend Press, pp. 279–309.

Fineman, Martha. (2005). *The Autonomy Myth*. The New Press.

Fisette, Jason. (2021). At the bar of conscience: a Kantian argument for slavery reparations. *Philosophy & Social Criticism*, *48*(5), 1–29.

Fleischacker, S. (1991). Philosophy in moral practice. *Kant-Studien, 82*(3), 249–69.

(1996). Values behind the market. *History of Political Thought, 17*(3), 379–407.

Flikschuh, Katrin. (2002). Kantian Desires. In Mark Timmons, ed., *Kant's Metaphysics of Morals: Interpretive Essays*. Oxford University Press, pp. 185–208.

Folbre, Nancy (2021). *The Rise and Decline of Patriarchal Systems*. Verso Books.

(2020). Manifold exploitations: toward an intersectional political economy. *Review of Social Economy, 78*(4), 451–72.

(1982). Exploitation comes home. *Journal of Economics, 6*(4), 317–29.

Fraser, Nancy. (2013). *Fortunes of Feminism*. Verso Books.

(1990). Rethinking the public sphere. *Social Text, 25/26*, 56–80.

Fraser, T., D. Aldrich, and C. Page-Tan, 2021. Bowling alone or distancing together? The role of social capital in excess death rates from COVID19. *Social Science & Medicine, 284*, 114241.

Gabriel, Mary. (2011). *Love and Capital*. Back Bay Books.

Gilman, Charlotte Perkins. (1898). *Women and Economics: A Study of the Economic Relation between Men and Women as a Factor in Social Evolution*. Small, Mayard & Co.

Gray, Marion. (2000). *Productive Men, Reproductive Women: The Agrarian Household and the Emergence of Separate Spheres during the German Enlightenment*. Berghahn Books.

Hartman, Saidiya. (2016). The belly of the world: a note on Black women's labors. *Souls, 18*(1), 166–73.

(1997). *Scenes of Subjection: Terror, Slavery, and Self-Making in Nineteenth-Century America*. Oxford University Press.

Hasan, Rafeeq. (2018). Freedom and poverty in the Kantian state. *European Journal of Philosophy, 26*(3), 911–31.

Hay, Carol. (2013). *Kantianism, Liberalism, and Feminism: Resisting Oppression*. Palgrave Macmillan.

Herman, Barbara. (1993). Can It Be Worth Thinking About Kant on Sex and Marriage? In Charlotte Witt, ed., *A Mind of One's Own: Feminist Essays on Reason and Objectivity*. Westview Press, pp. 49–67.

Hill Collins, Patricia (2002). *Black Feminist Thought: Knowledge, Consciousness, and the Politics of Empowerment*. Routledge.

(1989). The social construction of black feminist thought. *Signs: Journal of Women in Culture and Society, 14*(4), 745–73.

Holtman, Sarah. (2018). *Kant on Civil Society and Welfare*. Cambridge University Press.

(2004). Kantian Justice and Poverty Relief. *Kant-Studien*, *95*(1), 86–106.

Hochschild, Arlie (2001). Global Care Chains and Emotional Surplus Value. In Will Hutton and Anthony Giddens, eds, *On the Edge*. Vintage, pp. 130–46.

Hull, Isabel. (1997). *Sexuality, State, and Civil Society in Germany, 1700–1815*. Cornell University Press.

Huseyinzadegan, Dilek. (2019). *Kant's Nonideal Theory of Politics*. Northwestern University Press.

(2018). For what can the Kantian feminist hope? Constructive complicity in appropriations of the canon. *Feminist Philosophy Quarterly*, *4*(1), 1–26.

Huseyinzadegan, Dilek, and Jordan Pascoe. (Forthcoming). Feminist Disruptions of Enlightenment. In Susanne Lettow and Tuija Pulkinnen, eds, *The Palgrave Handbook of German Idealism and Feminist Philosophy*. Palgrave MacMillan.

(2021). Dismantling Kantian frames: notes towards a feminist politics of location and accountability. Blog of the APA, 7 April 2021. https://blog .apaonline.org/2021/04/07/dismantling-kantian-frames-notes-toward-a-feminist-politics-of-location-and-accountability/.

Jackson, Shona. (2014). Humanity beyond the regime of labor: antiblackness, indigeneity, and the legacies of colonialism in the Caribbean. *Decolonization: Indigeneity, Education & Society*. https://decolonization .wordpress.com/2014/06/06/humanity-beyond-the-regime-of-labor-anti blackness-indigeneity-and-the-legacies-of-colonialism-in-the-caribbean/.

(2012). *Creole Indigeneity: Between Myth and Nation in the Caribbean*. University of Minnesota Press.

Juhnke, W. E. (1974). Benjamin Franklin's View of the Negro and Slavery. *Pennsylvania History: A Journal of Mid-Atlantic Studies*, pp.375–89

King, Tiffany Lethabo. (2019). *The Black Shoals*. Duke University Press.

(2017). Humans involved: lurking in the lines of posthumanist flight. *Critical Ethnic Studies*, *3*(1), 162–85.

(2016). The labor of (re) reading plantation landscapes fungible(ly). *Antipode*, *48*(4), 1022–39.

Kirkland, Frank. (Forthcoming). Mills on Black radical Kantianism. *Kantian Review*.

Kleingeld, Pauline. (2019). On dealing with Kant's sexism and racism. *SGIR Review*, *2*(2), 3–22.

(2014a). Kant's Second Thoughts on Colonialism. In Katrin Flikschuh and Lea Ypi, eds, *Kant and Colonialism: Historical and Critical Perspectives*. Oxford University Press, pp. 43–67.

(2014b). *The Development of Kant's Cosmopolitanism*. University of Wales Press.

(2007). Kant's second thoughts on race. *The Philosophical Quarterly, 57*(229), 573–92.

(1993). The problematic status of gender-neutral language in the history of philosophy: the case of Kant. *Philosophical Forum, 25*(2), 134–50.

Kuhn, Manfred. (2001). *Kant: A Biography*. Cambridge University Press.

Langton, Rae, (2009). *Sexual Solipsism*. Oxford University Press.

Larrimore, Mark. (2008). Antinomies of race: diversity and destiny in Kant. *Patterns of Prejudice, 42*(4–5), 341–63.

Locke, John. (2015). *The Second Treatise of Civil Government*. Broadview Press.

Loriaux, Sylvie. (2020). *Kant and Global Distributive Justice*. Cambridge University Press.

Lu-Adler, Huaping. (2022a). Kant on slavery. *Critical Philosophy of Race 10*(2), 1–26.

(2022b). Kant on lazy savagery, racialized. *Journal of the History of Philosophy, 60*, 253–75.

Luft, Rachel E. (2016). Racialized disaster patriarchy: An intersectional model for understanding disaster ten years after Hurricane Katrina. *Feminist Formations*, 1–26.

Madrid, Nuria Sanchez. (2019). Poverty and civil recognition in Kant's juridical philosophy. *Revista Portuguesa de Filosofia, 75* (Fasc.1), 33–50.

Maliks, Reidar. (2014). *Kant's Politics in Context*. Oxford University Press.

Marx, Karl. (2005). *Early Writings*. Penguin Books.

(1976). *Capital*, vol. 1. Penguin Books.

Mendieta, Eduardo. (2011). Geography Is to History as Woman Is to Man. In Stuart Elden and Eduardo Mendieta, eds, *Reading Kant's Geography*. SUNY Press, pp. 345–67.

Mendus, Susan. (1992). *Kant: An Honest but Narrow-Minded Bourgeois*. Chicago University Press.

Mignolo, Walter. (2011). The Darker Side of the Enlightenment. In Stuart Elden and Eduardo Mendieta, eds, *Reading Kant's Geography*. SUNY Press, pp. 169–93.

Mills, Charles. (2017). Black radical Kantianism. *Res Philosophica, 95*(1), 1–33.

(2005). Kant's Untermenschen. In Andrew Valls, ed., *Race and Racism in Modern Philosophy*. Cornell University Press, pp. 169–93.

Miyamoto, Inez. 2020. 'COVID-19 healthcare workers: 70% are women'. Daniel K. Inouye Asia-Pacific Center for Security Studies. https://apcss .org/wp-content/uploads/2020/05/Security-nexus-COVID-19-Healthcare-Workers-miyamoto.pdf.

Moran, Kate. (2021). Kant on traveling blacksmiths and passive citizenship. *Kant-Studien, 112*(1), 105–26.

Murray, Melissa. (2008). The networked family. *Virginia Law Review, 94*(2), 385–455.

Murray, Pauli. 1970. The Liberation of Black Women. In Beverly Guy-Sheftall, ed., *Words of Fire: An Anthology of Black Feminist Thought*. New Press, pp. 186–98.

(1947). Why negro girls stay single. *Negro Digest 5*(9), 4–8.

Murray, Pauli, and M. Eastwood (1965). Jane Crow and the law. *George Washing Law Review, 34*(2), 232–56.

Muthu, Sankar. (2014). Productive Resistance in Kant's Political Thought. In Katrin Flikschuh and Lea Ypi, eds, *Kant and Colonialism: Historical and Critical Perspectives*. Oxford University Press, pp. 68–98.

Nussbaum, M. C., (1995). Objectification. *Philosophy & Public Affairs, 24*(4), 249–91.

Obinna, D. N., 2021. Essential and undervalued: health disparities of African American women in the COVID-19 era. *Ethnicity & Health, 26*(1), 68–79.

O'Neill, Onora. (1989). *Constructions of Reason: Explorations of Kant's Practical Philosophy*. Cambridge University Press.

Pallikkathayil, Japa. (2010). Deriving morality from politics: rethinking the formula of humanity. *Ethics, 121*(1), 16–47.

Papadaki, L. (2010). Kantian marriage and beyond. *Hypatia, 25*(2), 276–94.

(2007). Sexual objectification: from Kant to contemporary feminism. *Contemporary Political Theory, 6*(3), 330–48.

Pascoe, Jordan. (2019a). Rethinking race and gender in Kant: toward a non-ideal, intersectional Kant. *SGIR Review, 2*(2), 84–99.

(2019b). On finding yourself in a state of nature. *Feminist Philosophy Quarterly, 5*(3).

(2018). A Universal Estate? Why Kant's Account of Marriage Speaks to the 21st Century Debate. In Larry Krasnoff and Nuria Sanchez, eds, *Kant's Doctrine of Right in the Twenty First Century*. University of Wales Press, pp. 220–40.

(2017). Working women and monstrous mothers: Kant, Marx, and the valuation of domestic labour. *Kantian Review, 22*(4), 599–618.

(2015). Domestic labour, citizenship, and exceptionalism: rethinking Kant's 'woman problem'. *Journal of Social Philosophy, 46*(3), 340–56.

(2013). To love, honor, and contract: engagement and domesticity in Kant's *Rechtslehre*. *Women's Studies Quarterly, 41*(3), 195–209.

(2012). Patriarchalism and Enlightenment. In Ceasare Cuttica and Gaby Mahlberg, eds, *Patriarchal Moments*. Bloomsbury Academic Studies, pp. 115–22.

(2011). Personhood, protection, and promiscuity: some thoughts on Kant, mothers, and infanticide. *APA Newsletter on Feminist Philosophy, 10*(2), 4–7.

(Forthcoming b). Gender Politics: Using Feminist Moral and Epistemological Frameworks to Guide Decolonial Disaster Response. In Howard Williams, David Boucher, Peter Sutch, and David Reidy, eds, *The Palgrave Handbook of International Political Theory.* Palgrave MacMillan.

(2020). Surging solidarity: reorienting ethics for pandemics. *Kennedy Institute of Ethics Journal, 30*(3), 419–44.

Pateman, Carole, Charles Mills. (2007). *Contract and Domination.* Polity.

Ravano, Lorenzo. (2020). The borders of citizenship in the Haitian Revolution. *Political Theory, 49*(5), 717–42.

Ripstein, Arthur. (2010). *Force and Freedom.* Harvard University Press.

Rho, Hye Jin, Hayley Brown, and Shawn Fremstrad. (2020). A basic demographic profile of workers in frontline industries. Center for Economic and Policy Research. April 2020. https://cepr.net/wp-content/uploads/2020/04/2020-04-Frontline-Workers.pdf.Sabourin, Charlotte (2021). Kant's Enlightenment and women's peculiar immaturity. *Kantian Review, 26*(2), 235–60.

Sanford, Stella. (Forthcoming). The Taxonomy of 'Race' and the Anthropology of Sex. In Susanne Lettow and Tuija Pulkkinen, eds, *The Palgrave Handbook of German Idealism and Feminist Theory.* Palgrave.

Sarvasy, Wendy, and Patrizia Longo. (2004). The globalization of care. *International Feminist Journal of Politics, 6*(3), 392–415.

Schaff, K. (2001). Kant, political liberalism, and the ethics of same-sex relations. *Journal of Social Philosophy, 32*(3), 446–62.

Schapiro, Tamar. (1999). What is a child? *Ethics, 109*(4), 715–38.

Schott, Robin May. (1997). *Feminist Interpretations of Immanuel Kant.* Penn State Press.

Schroeder, Hannelore. (1997). Kant's Patriarchal Order. In Robin May Schott, ed., *Feminist Interpretations of Immanuel Kant.* Penn State Press, pp. 275–96.

Shell, S. M. (2016). Kant on Citizenship, Society, and Redistributive Justice. In Andrea Faggion, Alessandro Pinzani, and Nuria Sanchez Madrid, eds, *Kant and Social Policies.* Palgrave Macmillan, pp. 1–23.

Valdez, I. (2020). *Transnational Cosmopolitanism.* Cambridge University Press.

(2017). It's not about race: good wars, bad wars, and the origins of Kant's anti-colonialism. *American Political Science Review, 111*(4), 819–34.

Varden, Helga. (2020). *Sex, Love, and Gender: A Kantian Theory.* Oxford University Press.

(2018).Kant's Moral Theory and Feminist Ethics: Women, Embodiment, Care Relations, and Systemic Injustice. In Pieranna Garavaso, ed., *The Bloomsbury Companion to Analytic Feminism*. Bloomsbury, pp. 459–82.

(2014). Patriotism, poverty, and global justice: a Kantian engagement with Pauline Kleingeld's *Kant and Cosmopolitanism*. *Kantian Review*, *19*(2), 251–66.

(2012). A Kantian critique of the care tradition: family law and systemic justice. *Kantian Review*, *17*(2), 327–56.

(2008). Kant's non-voluntarist conception of political obligations. *Kantian Review*, *13*(2), 1–45.

(2006a). A Kantian conception of rightful sexual relations: sex, (gay) marriage, and prostitution. *Social Philosophy Today*, *22*, 199–218.

(2006b). Kant and dependency relations. *Dialogue: Canadian Philosophical Review/Revue canadienne de philosophie*, *45*(2), 257–84.

Weinrib, Jacob. (2008). Kant on citizenship and universal independence. *Australian Journal of Legal Philosophy*, *33*, 1–25.

(2002). Poverty and property in Kant's system of rights. *Notre Dame Law Review*, *78*, 795.

Wilderson III, F. B. (2010). *Red, White & Black*. Duke University Press.

Williams, Howard. (2006). Liberty, Equality, and Independence: Core Concepts in Kant's Political Philosophy. In Graham Bird, ed., *A Companion to Kant*. Blackwell Books, pp. 364–83.

(1983). *Kant's Political Philosophy*. Basil Blackwell.

(1977). Kant's concept of property. *The Philosophical Quarterly (1950-)*, *27*(106), 32–40.

Wolkowitz, Carol, Rachel Lara Cohen, Teela Sanders, and Kate Hardy, eds, *Body/Sex/Work: Intimate, Embodied and Sexualised Labour*. Macmillan International Higher Education, 2013.

Wood, Allen. (2017). Marx and Kant on capitalist exploitation. *Kantian Review*, *22*(4), 641–59.

(2016). Unjust exploitation. *The Southern Journal of Philosophy*, *54*, 92–108.

(1998). Kant's Historical Materialism. In Jane Kneller and Sidney Axinn, eds, *Autonomy and Community: Readings in Contemporary Kantian Social Philosophy*. State University of New York Press, pp. 15–38.

Wynter, Sylvia. (2003). Unsettling the coloniality of being/power/truth/freedom: towards the human, after man, its overrepresentation. *CR: The New Centennial Review*, *3*(3), 257–337.

(1992). Beyond the Categories of the Master Conception. In Paget Henry and Paul Buhle, eds, *CLR James's Caribbean*. Duke University Press, pp. 63–91.

Ypi, Lea. (2014). Kant's Philosophy of History. In Katrin Flikschuh and Lea Ypi, eds, *Kant and Colonialism: Historical and Critical Perspectives*. Oxford University Press, pp. 99–126.

Acknowledgements

I wish to thank Helga Varden, Dilek Huseyinzadegan, Elvira Basevich, Sarah Holtman, Mitch Stripling, Huaping Lu Adler, Sarah Clark Miller, and Howard Williams for their invaluable feedback on early drafts of this project, as well as Friedlande Sterling, Mitch Stripling, Olivia Stripling, Heather Yvonne Axford, Ryan Harsch, Laura Pascoe, John Haffner, Patsy and Charles Stripling, Peter Pascoe, Concepcion, and Jane Tekin for childcare and domestic labour support. I also owe a debt of gratitude to Frederick Rauscher for providing me with unpublished translations of Kant's early notes.

Cambridge Elements $\equiv$

The Philosophy of Immanuel Kant

Desmond Hogan
Princeton University
Desmond Hogan joined the philosophy department at Princeton in 2004. His interests include Kant, Leibniz and German rationalism, early modern philosophy, and questions about causation and freedom. Recent work includes 'Kant on the Foreknowledge of Contingent Truths', *Res Philosophica* 91 (1) (2014); 'Kant's Theory of Divine and Secondary Causation', in Brandon Look (ed.) *Leibniz and Kant*, Oxford University Press (2021); 'Kant and the Character of Mathematical Inference', in Carl Posy and Ofra Rechter (eds.) *Kant's Philosophy of Mathematics Vol. I*, Cambridge University Press (2020).

Howard Williams
University of Cardiff
Howard Williams was appointed Honorary Distinguished Professor at the Department of Politics and International Relations, University of Cardiff in 2014. He is also Emeritus Professor in Political Theory at the Department of International Politics, Aberystwyth University, a member of the Coleg Cymraeg Cenedlaethol (Welsh-language national college) and a Fellow of the Learned Society of Wales. He is the author of *Marx* (1980); *Kant's Political Philosophy* (1983); *Concepts of Ideology* (1988); *Hegel, Heraclitus and Marx's Dialectic* (1989); *International Relations in Political Theory* (1992); *International Relations and the Limits of Political Theory* (1996); *Kant's Critique of Hobbes: Sovereignty and Cosmopolitanism* (2003); *Kant and the End of War* (2012) and is currently editor of the journal Kantian Review. He is writing a book on the Kantian legacy in political philosophy for a new series edited by Paul Guyer.

Allen Wood
Indiana University
Allen Wood is Ward W. and Priscilla B. Woods Professor Emeritus at Stanford University. He was a John S. Guggenheim Fellow at the Free University in Berlin, a National Endowment for the Humanities Fellow at the University of Bonn and Isaiah Berlin Visiting Professor at the University of Oxford. He is on the editorial board of eight philosophy journals, five book series and The Stanford Encyclopedia of Philosophy. Along with Paul Guyer, Professor Wood is co-editor of The Cambridge Edition of the Works of Immanuel Kant and translator of the Critique of Pure Reason. He is the author or editor of a number of other works, mainly on Kant, Hegel and Karl Marx. His most recently published books are *Fichte's Ethical Thought*, Oxford University Press (2016) and *Kant and Religion*, Cambridge University Press (2020). Wood is a member of the American Academy of Arts and Sciences.

About the Series

This Cambridge Elements series provides an extensive overview of Kant's philosophy and its impact upon philosophy and philosophers. Distinguished Kant specialists provide an up-to-date summary of the results of current research in their fields and give their own take on what they believe are the most significant debates influencing research, drawing original conclusions.

Cambridge Elements ≡

The Philosophy of Immanuel Kant

Elements in the Series

A full series listing is available at: www.cambridge.org/EPIK

Printed in the United States
by Baker & Taylor Publisher Services